SAT®
VERBAL TESTS

✓

ADVANCED

PRACTICE
SERIES

◇ For the Redesigned SAT

◇ Full Tests and Scaled Scores

◇ Essential Tips and Tactics

ies

TEST
PREP

Authors
Arianna Astuni, President IES
Khalid Khashoggi, CEO IES

Editorial
Patrick Kennedy, Executive Editor
Christopher Carbonell, Editorial Director
Rajvi Patel, Editor
Caitlin Hoynes-O'Connor, Editor
Yasmine Gharib, Assistant Editor

Design
Kay Kang, www.kaygraphic.com

Contributors

Arianna Astuni	*Caitlin Hoynes-O'Connor*
Danielle Barkley	*Nathaniel Hunt*
Larry Bernstein	*Charles Kennedy*
Christopher Carbonell	*Patrick Kennedy*
Robert Collins	*Khalid Khashoggi*
Yasmine Gharib	*Paul King*
Cynthia Helzner	*Gabrielle Lenhard*
Nancy Hoffman	*Rajvi Patel*
Chris Holliday	*Cassidy Yong*

Published by IES Publications
www.IESpublications.com
© IES Publications, 2015

ON BEHALF OF
Integrated Educational Services, Inc.
355 Main Street
Metuchen, NJ 08840
www.ies2400.com

We would like to thank the IES Publications team as well as the teachers and students at IES2400 who have contributed to the creation of this book. We would also like to thank our Chief Marketing Officer, Sonia Choi, for her invaluable input.

The SAT® is a registered trademark of the College Board, which was not involved in the production of, and does not endorse, this product.

ISBN-10: 0-9964064-2-5
ISBN-13: 978-0-9964064-2-0
QUESTIONS OR COMMENTS? Visit us at ies2400.com

TABLE OF CONTENTS

Need an answer explained?
Visit ies2400.com/answers

To arrange group or private tutoring at one of our locations, please visit **ies2400.com** or e-mail us at **sat2400@ies2400.com**.

Your personal information will be kept confidential and will never be sold to third parties. IES may contact you periodically with special offers, updated information, and new services. Any e-mail sent by IES will provide the option to be removed from the e-mail mailing list.

Dear student,

When the College Board first announced that the SAT would be changing, we at IES began preparing for the new test as energetically and as conscientiously as possible. Now, we are past the March 2016 debut of the redesigned SAT and are entering a new era of practice and preparation. So far, many of the students I have spoken with are confident in their abilities, sure of their methods, and determined to achieve the best possible score. Yet one gap has remained in their SAT prep—accurate, relevant practice material. By now, many students have worked completely through the College Board's own book for the New SAT; these students need more of the kind of consistent, rigorous practice that is a key to success for any test taker.

If you are one of these students—determined to get the best preparation, devoted to your studies and your future—you are reading the ideal book. This latest volume in the IES Advanced Practice Series gives you control of the New SAT Verbal Section. You will find tests in both Reading and Grammar, along with special features that will lead you confidently forward—scaled scores, self-assessments, and online answer explanations at ies2400.com. And you will also benefit from our guarantee of excellence. Unlike the many books that appeared much too early in the game, this book is crafted using only the most recent information released by the College Board. The sample tests, question criteria, and design formats that were finalized in June 2015 have been our constant guides.

Delve into these tests and enhance your test-taking abilities. But make sure that you check back as the IES list of books continues to grow: already, a comprehensive New SAT Grammar book and a challenging New SAT Reading book are available, while several titles on New SAT Math are in the works. We know that you have the potential to achieve your target score—maybe even a perfect 1600. Make the most of this practice book, and make that potential a reality!

I wish you all the best in your test-taking endeavors.

Sincerely,

Arianna Astuni,
President, IES

New SAT
Essentials

The New Structure of the

SAT Verbal Test

Overview

Early in 2014, test-takers were alerted to major changes to both the SAT and the PSAT. The new version of the PSAT had its debut in October of 2015, while the new version of the SAT was administered for the first time in March of 2016. The New SAT and New PSAT only differ in a few ways (extra questions and an optional essay for the SAT), yet both of the redesigned tests depart radically from the earlier PSAT and SAT exams.

Here is a look at some of the major changes:

> ✔ **Remember**
>
> Despite changes in format, the SAT is still an evidence-based test. Other than relatively advanced vocabulary, you DO NOT need much specialized knowledge. Instead, you must focus on context clues and learn overarching strategies to succeed.

New SAT and PSAT	Old SAT and PSAT
Two multiple-choice subject areas (Verbal and Mathematics) and a maximum scaled score of 1600, with 800 as the maximum on each area. Optional SAT Essay section with a separate score.	Three multiple-choice subject areas (Verbal, Mathematics, and Grammar) and a maximum scaled score of 2400. Mandatory SAT Essay section combined with Grammar for a scaled Writing score out of 800.
Four answer choices, no guessing penalty.	Five answer choices, 0.25 point guessing penalty.
Reading section (part of Verbal) consisting entirely of five long reading comprehension passages.	Reading section (own 800 score) with sentence completions, short passages, and long passages.
Grammar section (part of Verbal) consisting entirely of four passages with accompanying error identification and passage editing questions.	Grammar section (combined with Essay for 800 score) with short questions on improving sentences, identifying sentence errors, and improving paragraphs.
Mathematics test consisting of one no-calculator section, one calculator-allowed section.	Mathematics test consisting of three sections, calculator use allowed throughout.
Graphics and visuals included for analysis and linked to questions in Reading and Grammar.	Graphics and visuals used only in the Mathematics sections.
Linked questions (analysis of a single chart or table, uses of evidence) in Reading and Mathematics	No directly and explicitly linked questions on any of the test sections.

New SAT Essentials

Reading Test

Each **Reading Test** will follow exactly the same positioning and roughly the same structure. Reading is the very first section that test-takers will encounter on the New SAT, and will always adhere to the following content and timing standards:

65 MINUTES to complete Five Passages

52 QUESTIONS at 10-11 Questions per Passage

The different passages themselves will also break down in a manner that should be familiar to test-takers well in advance:

♦   FIVE Passages per test, each passage between 500 and 750 words. The total word count for all passages will be 3250 words

♦   FOUR Topic Areas, which always occur in the following order: 1) Fiction, 2) Social Science, 3) Natural Science (first), 4) Global Conversation, 5) Natural Science (second)

♦   ONE Paired Passage reading and TWO Passages with graphics. A Paired Passage may occur in any of the Topic Areas except for Fiction; a graphic may occur in any of the Topic Areas except for Fiction and Global Conversation.

The Four Topic Areas for the New SAT Reading

Fiction: excerpts from novels and short stories, published between the eighteenth century and the present. The New SAT has prioritized written works that feature discernible conflicts or objectives and only a few principal characters.

Social Science: short essays and excerpts on economics, urban studies, transportation and infrastructure, careers and occupations, ethics and morality. A reading in this area will typically have a strong thesis supported by data, case studies, observed trends, and other evidence.

Natural Science: articles and excerpts discussing experiments and data, often with an emphasis on new knowledge or changing theories, in biology, chemistry, ecology, physics, astronomy, psychology, and related topics

Global Conversation: thesis-oriented documents, speeches, and excerpts from major politicians and important historical figures. These readings can range in date from the eighteenth to the twenty-first century.

> ✔ **Remember**
>
> When answering questions, always try to use effective process of elimination. Even if you ultimately need to guess on your answer, guessing between two decent-looking answers is better than randomly picking from four answers that you have not really examined.

Major Reading Question Types

Primary Purpose or Main Idea

These questions require you to give an accurate synopsis of the entire passage, often with a focus on the position or situation described.

Which choice best summarizes the passage?

A) A young man accepts a job that proves to be unexpectedly rewarding.

B) A young man achieves new insights by making a dramatic lifestyle change.

C) A young man deals with the whims of an unfair employer.

D) A young man questions the value and utility of his university education.

Content and Characterization

You may be asked, for these questions, to identify what is explicitly stated or asserted by the author. You may also need to give a summary of the tone of a portion of the passage.

Ms. Kurimoto addresses the narrator in a manner that can best be characterized as

A) bewildered.

B) cautious.

C) downcast.

D) amused.

Word in Context

For these questions, you will need to consider four possible meanings of a single word or phrase and decide which meaning is logically appropriate to the context given by the passage.

As used in line 16, "deliver" most nearly means

A) provide.

B) fulfill.

C) rescue.

D) transport.

Purpose, Function, and Developmental Pattern

These questions require attention to the fine points of device and structure, both for individual lines and for the passage as a whole.

The main purpose of the fifth paragraph (lines 45-57) is to

A) summarize an argument that the author rejects.

B) offer statistical evidence for an unpopular view.

C) describe an experiment that is inherently flawed.

D) question the methods used in a recent study.

Inference and Suggestion

Questions such as these require you to draw logical conclusions from passage content. Do NOT misread these as opportunities to interpret the passage or use outside knowledge.

Based on information in the passage, it can reasonably be inferred that the Goblin Shark

A) has only recently been studied by ecologists.

B) inhabits ecosystems that are difficult to explore.

C) has altered its behavior in response to natural disasters.

D) is of greater interest to non-specialists than to trained biologists.

Command of Evidence

Often linked to specific Content or Inference questions, Command of Evidence questions ask you to provide evidence for previous answers by choosing specific, justifying line references.

Which choice provides the best evidence for the answer to the previous question?

A) Lines 2-3 ("It was . . . statistics")

B) Lines 18-20 ("Despite such . . . Goblin Shark")

C) Lines 47-51 ("When Leary . . . Goblin Shark")

D) Lines 68-72 ("Ecologists . . . after all")

Graphics and Evidence

These questions may ask you to analyze a graphic (chart, table, map, diagram) on its own, or may ask you to compare the content of a graphic to the content of the passage it accompanies.

Do the data in the chart support the author's claims about "online merchandising" (line 39)?

A) Yes, because the data show that such merchandising is unregulated.

B) Yes, because the data indicate a proliferation of small online merchants.

C) No, because the data only account for merchants based in the United States.

D) No, because the data indicate a decrease in merchandising revenues.

New SAT Essentials

Grammar Test

Officially known as the **Writing and Language** test, this portion of the New SAT deals with grammar fundamentals such as verb tense, pronoun use, sentence structure, and standard English idioms. In addition, each Grammar Test will include questions on style, coherence, and the use of visual resources (charts, maps, tables, etc).

To succeed on the New SAT Grammar, you will need to work within the following time and content requirements in order to complete **four nonfiction passages**:

35 MINUTES to complete Four Passages

44 QUESTIONS at 11 Questions per Passage

On each Grammar test, you will need to answer questions for **four different passage types**. Each passage will be **400-450 words long**. The passage types will not always occur in the same order, but the passages themselves will always be written in similarly clear and informative styles. The four types are:

Careers: Passages that discuss work, employment, and related issues in culture and society. Workplace conditions, the economics of employment, changes to certain industries over time, the skills required for a certain career, and the modernization of older careers are all possible topics here.

> ✔ **Remember**
>
> After you determine the answer to a New SAT Grammar question, mentally slot your answer into the passage and read around for clarity and usage. If you are lost on a revision question, slot the revisions in and see which one is best; you might put yourself on track to the right answer.

Social Science: Similar in content to the Social Science passages found on the Reading Test. The major difference is that, in the Grammar Test, the passages in this topic category tend to survey situations, scenarios, and phenomena, rather than arguing strong theses or taking on highly personal tones.

Humanities: Passages that discuss issues in literature, visual art, the performing arts, philosophy, theater, hobbies, entertainment, and related areas. Some history passages will also be considered Humanities rather than Social Science.

Natural Science: Similar in content to the Natural Science passages found on the Reading Test. Due to space constraints, the author will often provide an overview of a scientific sub-field or describe a single experiment, rather than evaluating the perspectives and ramifications that are frequently of interest on the Reading Test.

Major Grammar Question Types

Essential Grammar Usage
Fundamental flaws in wording and syntax, including subject-verb disagreement, pronoun choice, adverb and adjective disagreement, and confusion involving contractions and possessives (it's/its, etc.)

because there was nine

cats in the basket.

8
A) NO CHANGE
B) there were
C) they was
D) they were

Sentence Structure
Overarching errors including parallelism, misplaced modifiers, comma splices, sentence fragments, standard phrases that use conjunctions, and improper comma and dash placement.

that it was not only

impressive but also

original.

9
A) NO CHANGE
B) and also original
C) but also it was original
D) and also it was original

Style and Concision
Departures from common English idioms, redundant phrases, excessively informal speech, improper diction (effect/affect, etc.), excessively wordy and non-concise phrasing.

were part of the annual

exhibition of 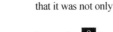 patterns

that were floral every year,

10
A) NO CHANGE
B) yearly floral patterns.
C) patterns, each year, and made with flowers.
D) floral patterns.

Topic and Coherence
Finding appropriate transitions from sentence to sentence and paragraph to paragraph, deciding which information is most relevant to the author's intent, theme, or argument.

unless you go to Russia

 and attend the

Moscow Circus for

yourself.

11
Which choice most effectively transitions from the previous paragraph?
A) NO CHANGE
B) as a member of a team of cultural anthropologists.
C) when the weather is relatively mild.
D) and avoid the difficulties I encountered.

Graphics and Response
Incorporating information from a graphic, deciding which reading of statistics is most accurate, deciding which information from a graphic is most relevant to the passage.

although the giant tapir

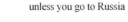 cannot accurately

discern objects more than

200 feet away.

12
Which choice offers the most accurate and relevant information from the data in the chart?
A) NO CHANGE
B) cannot accurately discern objects more than 100 feet away.
C) appears to have much sharper eyesight than the giant anteater.
D) appears to have much weaker eyesight than the giant anteater.

Ordering, Insertion, Deletion
Deciding whether to add or delete a sentence, where to place a new sentence, how to order sentences in a paragraph, how to order the paragraphs in a passage.

Question asks about the previous passage as a whole.

13
To make the passage most logical, paragraph 2 should be placed
A) where it is now.
B) before paragraph 1.
C) after paragraph 3.
D) after paragraph 4.

NEXT STEPS: Now that you know exactly what to expect on the New SAT, you will need consistent practice to become fully familiar with the test's material. Effective timing and excellent attention to detail are going to be your keys to success. If you need help, visit ies2400.com.

Test 1

Reading Test

65 MINUTES, 52 QUESTIONS

Turn to Section 1 of your answer sheet to answer the questions in this section.

DIRECTIONS

Each passage or pair of passages below is followed by a number of questions. After reading each passage or pair, choose the best answer to each question based on what is stated or implied in the passage or passages and in any accompanying graphics (such as a table or graph).

Questions 1-10 are based on the following passage.

Adapted from Thomas Hardy, *Jude the Obscure*, originally published in 1895. At this point in the narrative, the young Jude is living in a rural community and aspires to attend Christminster, a fictional British university that Hardy modeled on Oxford.

During the three or four succeeding years a quaint and singular vehicle might have been discerned moving along the lanes and by-roads near Marygreen, driven in a quaint and
Line singular way.
5   In the course of a month or two after the receipt of the books Jude had grown callous to the shabby trick played him by the dead languages. In fact, his disappointment at the nature of those tongues had, after a while, been the means of still further glorifying the erudition of Christminster. To acquire
10 languages, departed or living in spite of such obstinacies as he now knew them inherently to possess, was a herculean performance which gradually led him on to a greater interest in it than in the presupposed patent process. The mountain-weight of material under which the ideas lay in those dusty volumes
15 called the classics piqued him into a dogged, mouse-like subtlety of attempt to move it piecemeal.
He had endeavored to make his presence tolerable to his crusty maiden aunt by assisting her to the best of his ability, and the business of the little cottage bakery had grown in
20 consequence. An aged horse with a hanging head had been purchased for eight pounds at a sale, a creaking cart with a whity-brown tilt obtained for a few pounds more, and in this turn-out it became Jude's business thrice a week to carry loaves of bread to the villagers and solitary cotters immediately round
25 Marygreen.
The singularity aforesaid lay, after all, less in the

conveyance itself than in Jude's manner of conducting it along its route. Its interior was the scene of most of Jude's education by "private study." As soon as the horse had learned the road
30 and the houses at which he was to pause awhile, the boy, seated in front, would slip the reins over his arm, ingeniously fix open, by means of a strap attached to the tilt, the volume he was reading, spread the dictionary on his knees, and plunge into the simpler passages from Caesar, Virgil, or Horace, as
35 the case might be, in his purblind stumbling way, and with an expenditure of labor that would have made a tender-hearted pedagogue shed tears; yet somehow getting at the meaning of what he read, and divining rather than beholding the spirit of the original, which often to his mind was something else than
40 that which he was taught to look for.
The only copies he had been able to lay hands on were old Delphin editions, because they were superseded, and therefore cheap. But, bad for idle schoolboys, it did so happen that they were passably good for him. The hampered and lonely itinerant
45 conscientiously covered up the marginal readings, and used them merely on points of construction, as he would have used a comrade or tutor who should have happened to be passing by. And though Jude may have had little chance of becoming a scholar by these rough and ready means, he was in the way of
50 getting into the groove he wished to follow.
While he was busied with these ancient pages, which had already been thumbed by hands possibly in the grave, digging out the thoughts of these minds so remote yet so near, the bony old horse pursued his rounds, and Jude would be aroused from
55 the woes of Dido by the stoppage of his cart and the voice of some old woman crying, "Two today, baker, and I return this stale one."
He was frequently met in the lanes by pedestrians and others without his seeing them, and by degrees the people of
60 the neighborhood began to talk about his method of combining

CONTINUE

work and play (such they considered his reading to be), which, though probably convenient enough to himself, was not altogether a safe proceeding for other travelers along the same roads. There were murmurs. Then a private resident of an
65 adjoining place informed the local policeman that the baker's boy should not be allowed to read while driving, and insisted that it was the constable's duty to catch him in the act, and take him to the police court at Alfredston, and get him fined for dangerous practices on the highway. The policeman thereupon
70 lay in wait for Jude, and one day accosted him and cautioned him.

1

The passage is best described as

A) a humorous description of the downfall of a reckless young man.
B) an instructive tale about the dangers of excessive knowledge.
C) a light-hearted account of one individual's devotion to study.
D) a condemnation of the impracticality of dead languages.

2

It can be reasonably inferred that Jude is

A) a melancholy young man forced to deliver bread as punishment for an unnamed misdeed.
B) a poor young man with ambitions to dramatically alter his lifestyle.
C) an orphan with no aptitude for study or work.
D) a good-natured boy with little knowledge or conception of the world beyond his community.

3

As used in line 15, "piqued" most nearly means

A) confused.
B) irritated.
C) urged.
D) forced.

4

The first paragraph serves to anticipate the author's later discussion of

A) the intrinsic oddities of Marygreen.
B) Jude's unusual driving habits.
C) the dangers of traveling along country roads in late nineteenth-century England.
D) the delays and mishaps involved in the delivery of Jude's books.

5

Which choice provides the best evidence for the answer to the previous question?

A) Lines 9-13 ("To acquire . . . patent process")
B) Lines 17-20 ("He had . . . in consequence")
C) Lines 26-29 ("The singularity . . . private study")
D) Lines 43-44 ("But, bad . . . good for him")

6

As used in line 31, "ingeniously" most nearly means

A) resourcefully.
B) brilliantly.
C) imaginatively.
D) cunningly.

7

The passage most strongly suggests that Jude's studies "would have made a tender-hearted pedagogue shed tears" (lines 36-37) because

A) Jude applied a great deal of effort to understanding the texts.
B) Jude habitually misinterpreted even the simplest passages to a point of nonrecognition.
C) Jude approached his studies in a lazy and haphazard way.
D) Jude excelled in the interpretation of Latin texts to an extent that would impress established teachers.

8

It is reasonable to conclude that Jude's studies were

A) sufficient to establish his academic credentials.
B) worthless except for the diversion they provided the townspeople.
C) valuable insofar as they set him along the path that he desired.
D) of immense importance in helping him to understand human nature.

9

Which choice provides the best evidence for the answer to the previous question?

A) Lines 7-9 ("In fact . . . Christminster")
B) Lines 29-37 ("As soon . . . tears")
C) Lines 48-50 ("And though . . . follow")
D) Lines 64-69 ("Then a . . . highway")

10

It can be reasonably inferred that "Dido" (line 55) is

A) an educated woman from Jude's earlier years.
B) a nickname given to Jude's aunt.
C) a character from one of Jude's books.
D) an idealized figure from Jude's own imagination.

Questions 11-20 are based on the following passage and supplementary material.

Written by a specialist in higher education, this passage considers the career prospects of college and university students who have majored in the humanities.

Fields of study that have often been characterized as completely impractical—literature, art history, philosophy—have been getting a lot of positive press lately. The standard
Line line that such press takes goes something like this: over the past
5 two decades, advanced economies focused overwhelmingly on skills in quantitative analysis and produced an over-abundance of engineers, data analysts, and investment bankers. What weren't produced were enough students and professionals with exceptional written, spoken, and interpersonal aptitudes.
10 Yet these aptitudes, which are actually fostered by those "impractical" disciplines, are what employers need in an increasingly large and complex world economy. There are more than enough college graduates who can crunch numbers; there aren't enough who can sit a client down and effectively explain
15 why those numbers matter.
Perhaps the best exemplification of this standard line is a 2013 article entitled "Why English Majors Are the Hot New Hires," written by entrepreneurship and leadership specialist Bruna Martinuzzi. Long satirized as the most otherworldly of
20 all otherworldly fields, college-level English, in Martinuzzi's view, is instead a passport to a set of skills that employers crave: most obviously, good writing and coherent critical thinking; somewhat less obviously, exceptional sympathy and empathy. According to Martinuzzi, one basic online search

Desired Applicant Qualifications Based on Employer Listings

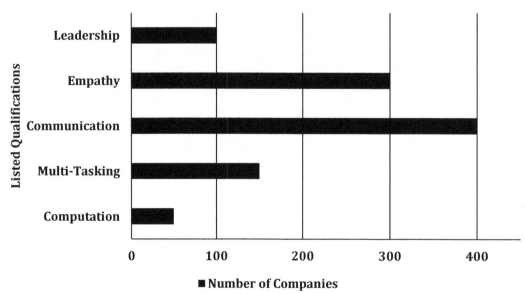

■ Number of Companies

CONTINUE

25 of monthly job postings returned "over 1,000 listings for highly paid jobs where employers list empathy as a necessary qualification. And these were not just jobs in traditionally compassionate sectors, such as health care and nonprofits; they included companies in technology, finance, consulting and
30 aerospace, to name a few."

You can't argue with hard numbers, but you can argue with the wisdom of some of the conclusions they have yielded. Most obvious is something of an inconsistency in sheer cause and effect: the average English major studies English to become
35 a scholar, teacher, or professor of English, not an aerospace consultant. And for those in English and other characteristically impractical disciplines who do leave academia and enter the commanding heights of the world economy, the journey involves far more than responding to a few employer listings.

40 A somewhat more accurate explanation of what really happens has recently been furnished by cultural anthropologist and Memling Institute Fellow Amanda Flock. "Students in the humanities," notes Flock, "do not programmatically absorb the skills that make them into successful businessmen
45 or entrepreneurs." What they absorb, instead, are what Flock calls "side-effect skills." The average English major, for instance, will sit down to read Jane Austen's *Emma* with the aim of understanding Austen's narrative devices, approach to characterization, and perspective on society. As the side effect
50 of such analysis—not its original intention—that English major will probably learn a thing or two about human nature and good decision making, or about other business fundamentals. Such skills manifest themselves especially well under duress: an English major, for instance, may leave college, find no jobs
55 within the field of literature, fall on his or her resources of personality, and improvise a way to employment.

These side-effect skills can be enormously potent, if that English major is ever nudged out of academia. More likely, that English major has signed up for a lifetime of reading
60 and re-reading Jane Austen. Desirable though they may be, humanities students find themselves secured within small circles of humanists, partially as the result of hard economics. On average, students in engineering and business come from lower-income households than students in the humanities
65 do. On average as well, mid-career engineers, architects, and statisticians make $30,000 more per year than do their counterparts in English, philosophy, history, and theater. Those who study the humanities aren't setting out to take control of the job market or even to out-earn their parents. It is more
70 likely, in a large number of cases, that they just need enough money to remain comfortably impractical.

11

Which choice best describes the structure of this passage?

A) A description of a trend followed by an argument as to the danger of that trend

B) A generalization about a group that is refuted by a deeper analysis of that group

C) A description of a changing attitude that leads into a critical analysis of that change

D) A defense of a phenomenon that is substantiated by a rigorous analysis of the national economy

12

The author of the passage introduces "The standard line" in lines 3-4 in order to

A) disprove a dangerous myth about the composition of the workforce.

B) support a later claim regarding the economic desirability of humanities majors.

C) introduce a popular claim that will be openly critiqued later in the passage.

D) focus on the unreliability of those who advise students on choosing courses of study.

13

Which choice provides the best evidence for the answer to the previous question?

A) Lines 19-24 ("Long satirized . . . empathy")

B) Lines 32-36 ("Most obvious . . . consultant")

C) Lines 46-49 ("The average . . . on society")

D) Lines 67-69 ("Those who . . . parents")

14

As used in line 43, "programmatically" most nearly means

A) methodically.

B) confidently.

C) punctually.

D) exhaustively.

15

The author of this passage suggests that humanities majors are most likely to leave academia when

A) they are provided financial incentives above and beyond those provided by academic positions.

B) they are recruited by employment agencies for large corporations.

C) they fail to find positions with academic sectors.

D) they realize the high value of their interpersonal skills.

16

Which choice provides the best evidence for the answer to the previous question?

A) Lines 12-15 ("There are . . . matter")

B) Lines 27-30 ("And these . . . few")

C) Lines 53-56 ("Such skills . . . . employment")

D) Lines 65-67 ("On average . . . theater")

17

It can be inferred that the employers surveyed in the graph would generally respond to the ideas put forward by Bruna Martinuzzi with

A) agreement, because humanities curricula include direct study of interpersonal skills such as empathy and sympathy.

B) agreement, because the skills Martinuzzi cites directly are in higher demand than qualities such as computation and multi-tasking.

C) disagreement, because strong leadership aptitude is a necessary prerequisite for attaining the empathy and communication skills that Martinuzzi values.

D) disagreement, because all business sectors, not just traditionally compassionate ones, can use the skills of English majors.

18

The author mentions *Emma* as an example of a book that

A) communicates valuable lessons about human behavior.

B) epitomizes the frivolous studies of English students.

C) remains one of the best guides to successful business practices in the literary canon.

D) disproves Flock's characterization of humanities studies.

19

The author refers to the comparative incomes of the families of humanities and science majors in order to

A) argue that science majors face more significant obstacles to success.

B) explain that humanities students tend to be less financially ambitious than those who study science.

C) observe that humanities majors are ultimately unlikely to exceed their parents in income.

D) refute the misconception that students of the humanities come from relatively disadvantaged backgrounds.

20

Which of the following can be reasonably concluded from the passage and from the data in the graph?

A) College students with strong interpersonal skills are generally uninterested in developing similarly strong computation skills.

B) Most college graduates fail to develop the leadership skills that are necessary in high-paying jobs.

C) Computation skills are currently a lower priority for employers than these skills were in the past.

D) Employers are likely to place a renewed emphasis on multi-tasking and a lowered emphasis on communication over the next few years.

20

Questions 21-30 are based on the following passages.

Recently, increased study of epidemic diseases has been prompted by crises in public health. The authors of the two passages below consider issues in the history of medicine; the first passage is from an article on intellectual history published in 1998, while the second article is from an editorial that appeared in an American newspaper in 2014.

Passage 1

The word "plague" has always created fear in the human soul; it makes us aware not only of our own mortality, but also of that of our race. Indeed, there have been periods in history when
Line human extinction has seemed quite possible. In the Middle Ages,
5 "the Black Death"—which we now know as Bubonic plague— was carried by black rats and spread throughout Europe, claiming the lives of between 30% and 50% of the population. In 1918, the "Spanish" Flu pandemic claimed more lives than had been taken by the violence of the First World War. At the time,
10 these contagions, silently arriving and claiming their victims, appeared to be unstoppable and, so it seemed, beyond the control of mere mortals. It was as if all of civilization felt powerless in the face of the inevitable.

Yet in 1796, Dr. Edward Jenner first created the hope that
15 there might be a means of controlling, and even of eradicating, such devastating diseases. Jenner's engineering of the first effective vaccine against smallpox led to the belief, now commonly held, that all plagues could eventually be defeated. This eighteenth-century success emboldened scientists to
20 explore the origins of what were previously assumed to be intractable afflictions. For example, by examining the water supplies in areas where cholera was rampant, scientists gained the knowledge necessary to treat this disease. Studying the disease at its source was of paramount importance, yet such
25 study would not have been attempted without the heartening success of Jenner's discoveries. Thanks to the pioneering efforts of Dr. Jenner, the dogged courage of scientific exploration has continued unabated, showing us that it is possible to control and eradicate what earlier civilizations regarded as incurable
30 contagions. As a result, vaccination is now commonplace. The world is a safer place for it.

Passage 2

Just because one has the right tool for the job does not necessarily mean that one will use it. If my air conditioner is broken, for example, and I have the right pair of pliers to
35 tackle the task at hand, you can rest assured that I will get to work; my comfort and my well-being are directly at stake. However, if another man on the other side of town has a broken air conditioner, and has no pliers to fix it, I might not be immediately inclined to help. After all, I don't live in that man's
40 house. Depending on the news coverage, I might not even be aware of that man's plight. What difference does it make to me?

As self-interested and complacent as this might sound, it is a common public attitude towards the ever-growing threat of the devastating Ebola virus, which made headlines after
45 a recent, high-drama outbreak. To be fair, our indifference is understandable. Due to the astounding successes of such medical advances as the development of smallpox and polio vaccines, which all but eradicated those diseases from the face of the earth, we tend to feel secure in our knowledge that there is no disease
50 that cannot be cured by science. And while this certainly may be the case, the indisputable fact remains that no disease will ever be cured without real research and serious effort.

We must remind ourselves that the vaccines for smallpox and polio did not come out of thin air, and did not appear
55 simply because scientists willed them to; these measures were developed through hard work and toil. We cannot presume that, thanks to the scientific breakthroughs of the past, we will forever be healthy and safe. As we all know, the world grows smaller by the day; with daily trans-Atlantic flights from West Africa to
60 New York City, we cannot afford to act as though Ebola exists elsewhere, in an alternate universe that cannot affect us. After all, this is not just a case of a broken air conditioner, but a very real and dangerous disease that could potentially land on our very doorstep. As a developed nation at the forefront of medical
65 science, it is necessary for us to devote our considerable energy and resources to confronting Ebola at its source—in the West African nations where it grows more threatening by the day. Only then will we stand a chance of eradicating this disease, just as our forebears eradicated smallpox and polio.

21

The author of Passage 1 is best described as

A) a proponent of scientific research.

B) a scholar criticizing a particular use of terminology.

C) a historian revealing modern misconceptions.

D) a writer reflecting on a personal experience.

22

Which choice provides the best evidence for the answer to the previous question?

A) Lines 1-3 ("The word . . . race")

B) Lines 14-16 ("Yet in . . . diseases")

C) Lines 16-18 ("Jenner's . . . defeated")

D) Lines 26-30 ("Thanks to . . . contagions")

23

As used in line 30, "commonplace" most nearly means

A) approachable.

B) uninteresting.

C) overused.

D) widespread.

24

Both passages are primarily concerned with the issue of

A) public health.

B) incurable diseases.

C) scientific controversy.

D) global economics.

25

The author of Passage 1 does which of the following to suggest that vaccination was revolutionary?

A) Details the political upheaval that followed a medical breakthrough

B) Describes the power of disease prior to the discovery of vaccination

C) Compares modern medical techniques to those from the Middle Ages

D) Implies that humans are no longer required to worry about their own mortality

26

The author of Passage 2 most likely mentions an air conditioner in order to

A) add humor to an otherwise somber debate.

B) elaborate on an earlier statement.

C) differentiate two likely threats.

D) explain why certain technologies are unnecessary.

27

The author of Passage 2 refers to trans-Atlantic flights (line 59) primarily to

A) imply that anyone in the world could easily contract Ebola.

B) suggest that people who lived centuries ago were safer than people today.

C) substantiate the claim that diseases can spread rapidly.

D) provide an unexpected example of a positive effect of modernization.

28

As used in line 67, "grows" most nearly means

A) becomes.

B) sprouts.

C) flourishes.

D) augments.

29

Like the author of Passage 1, the author of Passage 2 would agree with which of the following statements?

A) The increasing mobility of the public poses a challenge to those trying to contain disease.

B) Triumphing over Ebola will require years of serious medical research.

C) The advent of vaccination has made people less fearful of disease.

D) The public has become too relaxed about the prospect of a modern epidemic.

30

Which choice provides the best evidence for the answer to the previous question?

A) Lines 32-33 ("Just because . . . use it")

B) Lines 46-50 ("Due to the . . . by science")

C) Lines 53-56 ("We must . . . and toil")

D) Lines 64-67 ("As a . . . day")

CONTINUE

Questions 31-41 are based on the following passage.

This passage is adapted from a speech delivered by William Lloyd Garrison on February 14, 1854, to the Broadway Tabernacle in New York. In the passage, Garrison discusses slavery in the United States and the abolitionist movement.

Notwithstanding the lessons taught us by Pilgrim Fathers and Revolutionary Sires, at Plymouth Rock, on Bunker Hill, at Lexington, Concord and Yorktown; notwithstanding our Fourth
Line of July celebrations, and ostentatious displays of patriotism; in
5 what European nation is personal liberty held in such contempt as in our own? Where are there such unbelievers in the natural equality and freedom of mankind?

Our slaves outnumber the entire population of the country at the time of our revolutionary struggle. In vain do they clank
10 their chains, and fill the air with their shrieks, and make their supplications for mercy. In vain are their sufferings portrayed, their wrongs rehearsed, their rights defended. As Nero fiddled while Rome was burning, so the slaveholding spirit of this nation rejoices, as one barrier of liberty after another is destroyed, and
15 fresh victims are multiplied for the cotton-field and the auction-block.

For one impeachment of the slave system, a thousand defences are made. For one rebuke of the man-stealer, a thousand denunciations of the Abolitionists are heard. For one press that
20 bears a faithful testimony against Slavery, a score are ready to be prostituted to its service. For one pulpit that is not "recreant to its trust," there are ten that openly defend slaveholding as compatible with Christianity, and scores that are dumb. For one church that excludes the human enslaver from its communion
25 table, multitudes extend to him the right hand of religious fellowship.

The wealth, the enterprise, the literature, the politics, the religion of the land, are all combined to give extension and perpetuity to the Slave Power. Everywhere to do homage
30 to it, to avoid collision with it, to propitiate its favour, is deemed essential—nay, is essential to political preferment and ecclesiastical advancement. Nothing is so unpopular as impartial liberty. The two great parties which absorb nearly the whole voting strength of the Republic are pledged to be deaf, dumb
35 and blind to whatever outrages the Slave Power may attempt to perpetrate. Cotton is in their ears—blinds are over their eyes— padlocks are upon their lips. They are as clay in the hands of the potter, and already moulded into vessels of dishonour, to be used for the vilest purposes.
40 The tremendous power of the Government is actively wielded to "crush out" the little Anti-Slavery life that remains in individual hearts, and to open new and boundless domains for the expansion of the Slave system. No man known or suspected to be hostile to "the Compromise Measures, including the

45 Fugitive Slave Law," is allowed to hope for any office under the present Administration. The ship of State is labouring in the trough of the sea—her engine powerless, her bulwarks swept away, her masts gone, her lifeboats destroyed, her pumps choked, and the leak gaining rapidly upon her; and as wave after
50 wave dashes over her, all that might otherwise serve to keep her afloat is swallowed by the remorseless deep. God of heaven! if the ship is destined to go down "full many a fathom deep," is every soul on board to perish? Ho! a sail! a sail! The weather-beaten, but staunch ship Abolition, commanded by the Genius
55 of Liberty, is bearing toward the wreck, with the cheering motto, inscribed in legible capitals, "WE WILL NOT FORSAKE YOU!" Let us hope, even against hope, that rescue is not wholly impossible.

To drop what is figurative for the actual, I have expressed
60 the belief that, so lost to all self-respect and all ideas of justice have we become by the corrupting presence of Slavery, in no European nation is personal liberty held at such discount, as a matter of principle, as in our own.

31

The stance Garrison takes in the passage is best described as that of

A) a critic of the status quo.

B) an advocate for nationalistic principles.

C) an opponent of political revolution.

D) a scholar of African-American history.

32

Based on the passage, which choice best describes how Garrison feels about slavery?

A) It will inevitably be abolished by the United States.

B) It is more accepted in Europe than in the United States.

C) It has only continued for economic reasons in the United States.

D) It has degraded the founding principles of the United States.

33

Which choice provides the best evidence for the answer to the previous question?

A) Lines 9-11 ("In vain . . . mercy")

B) Lines 23-26 ("For one . . . fellowship")

C) Lines 40-43 ("The tremendous . . . Slave system")

D) Lines 59-63 ("I have . . . own")

CONTINUE 23

34

The main rhetorical effect of the third paragraph
(lines 17-26) is to

A) suggest that abolitionists face insurmountable challenges.

B) convey the threat that the slave system poses to democracy.

C) show that abolitionists are outnumbered by those who support slavery.

D) indicate that slavery is a system that denies individuals their inalienable rights.

35

As used in line 20, "bears" most nearly means

A) approaches.

B) produces.

C) receives.

D) endures.

36

In his speech, Garrison does which of the following to argue against slavery?

A) Explains how abolition will restore the strength of the current government administration

B) Implies that Americans do not live by the ideals that they celebrate

C) Compares the accomplishments of freed slaves to those of other Americans

D) Details the daily tortures and injustices suffered by slaves

37

Which choice provides the best evidence for the answer to the previous question?

A) Lines 1-6 ("Notwithstanding the . . . our own?")

B) Lines 8-9 ("Our slaves . . . struggle")

C) Lines 27-29 ("The wealth . . . Power")

D) Lines 43-46 ("No man . . . Administration")

38

As used in line 33, "absorb" most nearly means

A) captivate.

B) acquire.

C) understand.

D) encompass.

39

Lines 46-51 ("The ship . . . deep") serve primarily to

A) explain the similarities between a country and a ship.

B) highlight the state's resilience.

C) dramatize the nation's peril.

D) vilify the current administration.

40

It can be reasonably inferred from the passage that politicians are generally

A) candid about their objectives.

B) independent and unbiased thinkers.

C) subject to abolitionist influence.

D) responsive to popular opinion.

41

In the passage, Garrison establishes a contrast between

A) the aggressive influence of Slave Power and the passive compliance of society.

B) the cautiousness of American historical figures and the assertiveness of the Abolitionists.

C) the good work done by the Government and the injustice of the Compromise Measures.

D) the duplicity of American political parties and the honesty of European politicians.

CONTINUE

Questions 42-52 are based on the following passage and supplementary material.

The following passage is excerpted from an article about whale evolution.

In a space of only fifty million years, whales have evolved from four-legged land animals into the wonderful aquatic creatures they are today. Relative to the evolution of other life
Line forms, the whale's is fast. The sharks we see swimming around
5 us have remained the same for over 350 million years, though they are, as we all are, in a process of slow evolutionary change.
We may not know exactly why or how one species evolves faster than another, but we can certainly identify climate change and dwindling food supplies as primary causes. Fossils of the
10 now-extinct Pakicetus, recently discovered in sedimentary rock formations, have elucidated some of the mysteries surrounding the whale's departure from land. This earliest-known ancestor of the whale walked around on four legs and sported a tail. It was approximately the size of a wolf. Evidence from the geologic
15 record surrounding these fossils reveals that there was an abrupt increase in global temperature at the time Pakicetus was alive. This leads us to believe that its regular food supply may have been abruptly altered, forcing Pakicetus to forage for food in the water. Fifty million years later, after several transitional phases
20 of evolution, Pakicetus became the blue whale, the humpback, the dolphin, and all other members of the cetacean order. Unlike many of the life forms that became extinct (think dinosaur) the whales are successful at responding to drastic environmental change.
25 And they are still evolving.
In the mid 1980s, an unusual sound was picked up by scientists. It bore the signature of a whale song and was detected along well-documented migration routes used by whales, but it was at a frequency of 52 Hertz, which is significantly outside the
30 15-20 Hertz range used by, and audible to, whales. This sound has been monitored and studied over three decades. No sighting of any animal responsible for this sound has ever been made, but marine biologists are certain of one fact: this is the sound of a whale that has no friends. No other whale activity has ever been
35 recorded in the vicinity of or in response to this sound. Biologists have dubbed the creature emitting the sound "Whale 52." Different theories have emerged in the attempt to explain this phenomenon. Some have posited that Whale 52 is a hybrid, or a deformed, or a deaf whale. But what if this is a perfectly healthy
40 animal, the newest specimen of whale evolution?
Indeed, the home of the whale was transformed overnight by Man. We arrived on the scene only two million years ago and became significant to whales only in the last one hundred years: our rapid and formidable technological evolution has given rise
45 to underwater noise pollution through submarine sonar activity, nuclear bomb testing, and incessant pings from scientific devices

that measure everything in the oceans. These disturbances are believed to be responsible for the disorientation of whales that rely on sound for their own survival. Whale songs are thought to
50 function on multiple levels: courtship, navigation, food sourcing. By interfering with the natural processes of reproduction, migration, and feeding, our artificial underwater sounds may be spurring the latest phase of the whale's evolution. After all, we are altering their environment and they have proven able to
55 respond rapidly.

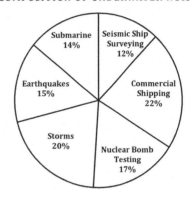

Figure 1
COMPOSITION OF UNDERWATER NOISE

Submarine 14%
Seismic Ship Surveying 12%
Earthquakes 15%
Commercial Shipping 22%
Storms 20%
Nuclear Bomb Testing 17%

Figure 2

Country	Dead or Beached Whales with Brain or Inner Ear Injuries, 2013 (%)
Bahamas	47
Greece	72

Figure 1 and Figure 2 are adapted from the Oceanic Preservation Society website, www.opsociety.org. Figure 1 depicts underwater noise and Figure 2 provides data for autopsied whales that died from injuries associated with intense underwater sound.

42

The author refers to "fifty million years" in the first paragraph primarily to

A) introduce a thesis about whale evolution.

B) note a particularly long evolutionary history.

C) outline an implausible scientific theory.

D) assess the relative physical strength of two species.

43

The passage most strongly suggests that evolution occurs as a direct result of

A) genetic variation and selective pressure.

B) migrations and anatomical transformations.

C) a changing environment and food scarcity.

D) the passage of time and foraging behavior.

44

Which choice provides the best evidence for the answer to the previous question?

A) Lines 4-5 ("The sharks . . . years")

B) Lines 7-9 ("We may . . . causes")

C) Lines 12-13 ("This earliest-known . . . a tail")

D) Lines 19-21 ("Fifty million . . . order")

45

As used in line 27, "bore" most nearly means

A) held up.

B) wore.

C) assumed.

D) exhibited.

46

The author's attitude towards whales could best be described as

A) appreciative.

B) amused.

C) perplexed.

D) disappointed.

47

Which choice provides the best evidence for the answer to the previous question?

A) Lines 13-14 ("It was . . . wolf")

B) Lines 23-24 ("the whales . . . change")

C) Lines 38-39 ("Some have . . . whale")

D) Lines 49-50 ("Whale songs . . . sourcing")

48

As used in line 36, "dubbed" most nearly means

A) copied.

B) named.

C) mimicked.

D) soothed.

49

Based on the passage, which statement best describes the human impact on whale species?

A) Our relatively new technology has quickly altered the environment in which the whales operate.

B) Our disruption of whale communication will eventually eliminate the entire whale population.

C) The noise pollution that we have created is forcing whales to communicate more effectively.

D) The effects of our development are negligible when compared to the long history of the whale species.

50

Based on Figure 1 and the passage, which choice gives the correct percentages of underwater noise that does NOT contribute to the disorientation of whales?

A) 15% and 12%

B) 20% and 15%

C) 22% and 17%

D) 14% and 12%

CONTINUE

51

Which choice is supported by the data in the second figure?

A) A large percentage of Greece's coastline is inhabited by whales.

B) The number of whales that suffered injury is highest near the Bahamas.

C) The percentage of whales with recorded injuries is highest near Greece.

D) The number of whales that suffered injury is roughly the same for Greece and the Bahamas.

52

Based on the two figures, the author would most likely conclude which of the following?

A) Whales near the Bahamas are less affected by human-sourced underwater noise pollution than those near Greece.

B) Whales near the Bahamas will be more likely to survive natural disasters than those near Greece.

C) Greece's thriving fishing industry accounts for its underwater noise pollution.

D) The volume of commercial shipping is lower in the Bahamas than in Greece.

STOP

If you finish before time is called, you may check your work on this section only.
Do not turn to any other section.

Writing Test

35 MINUTES, 44 QUESTIONS

Turn to Section 2 of your answer sheet to answer the questions in this section.

DIRECTIONS

Each passage below is accompanied by a number of questions. For some questions, you will consider how the passage might be revised to improve the expression of ideas. For other questions, you will consider how the passage might be edited to correct errors in sentence structure, usage, or punctuation. A passage or a question may be accompanied by one or more graphics (such as a table or graph) that you will consider as you make revising and editing decisions.

Some questions will direct you to an underlined portion of a passage. Other questions will direct you to a location in a passage or ask you to think about the passage as a whole.

After reading each passage, choose the answer to each question that most effectively improves the quality of writing in the passage or that makes the passage conform to the conventions of standard written English. Many questions include a "NO CHANGE" option. Choose that option if you think the best choice is to leave the relevant portion of the passage as it is.

Questions 1-11 are based on the following passage.

The Gist of Pipilotti Rist

Pipilotti Rist is a Swedish video artist **1** that has been producing work since the late 1980's. She studied video **2** by the School of Design in Basel, Switzerland. Over the course of her career, Rist has exhibited in both group and solo shows across the globe. Her artwork **3** focused on images of women and objects associated with women, such as flowers and makeup. Electric hues of pink and purple regularly color her films, while the individual images often appear to be softened.

1
A) NO CHANGE
B) who
C) whom
D) whose

2
A) NO CHANGE
B) for
C) at
D) with

3
A) NO CHANGE
B) focuses on
C) focusing on
D) focuses into

CONTINUE

[1] In 2008, Rist exhibited at the Museum of Modern Art in New York City. [2] Installed in the museum's atrium, Rist's show consisted of a sixteen-minute film played on a loop. [3] The effect was immersive, almost as though the viewer had been placed at the bottom of a bowl. [4] In this way, Rist created an artistic womb in which to nurture the museum's visitors. ■4

Unlike passive and uninterested television spectators, Rist's viewers actively choose to bring themselves into her art. Thus, to accommodate her audience, Rist routinely transforms the physical spaces of her installations into areas that viewers can comfortably ■5 inhabit. Her 2011 exhibit at the Australian Centre for Contemporary Art, *I Packed the Postcard in My Suitcase*, demonstrates this idea. ■6 So, Rist projected her videos both onto the ceiling and onto arranged piles of fabric on the floor. Viewers could lie down and absorb the images, which drifted by like passing clouds.

4

Where is the most logical place in this paragraph to add the following sentence?

> Due to the scale of the projection, the viewer was surrounded by floor-to-ceiling images on all sides.

A) After sentence 1
B) After sentence 2
C) After sentence 3
D) After sentence 4

5

A) NO CHANGE
B) inhibit.
C) habitat.
D) exhibit.

6

Which choice provides the most logical introduction to the sentence?
A) NO CHANGE
B) But,
C) Consequently,
D) There,

Some critics found the warmth of the environment generated by *I Packed the Picture in My Suitcase*, and the pleasantry of Rist's imagery, to be cloyingly friendly. But pleasantry is not a prevailing state for Rist. Rather than providing mellow sensations all the time, she has actively challenged contemporary culture; she appropriates videos from mass media and uses a great deal of popular and contemporary music in her pieces. Her video *Sip My Ocean*, **7** then, is set to an interpretation of Chris Isaac's pop song "Wicked Game." **8** This whimsical tactic likens her to a producer of experimental music.

Rist's awareness of popular culture is complemented by her participation in the intellectual or "conceptual" turn that art-making has recently taken. **9** Increasingly the concept, or idea behind the creation of artwork supersedes that idea's physical manifestation. The Rist video *Open My Glade (Flatten)* depicts a blonde woman, her body bare from the shoulders up. She is heavily made up with red lipstick and blue eye shadow. She **10** stood before a pane of glass and proceeds to rub her face back and forth across it, streaking it with makeup. Here, **11** Rist records the creation of something emotional and visceral, rather than distantly ideological or academic. She makes art accessible to the viewer.

7
A) NO CHANGE
B) therefore,
C) also,
D) for example,

8
Which choice most effectively concludes the paragraph?
A) NO CHANGE
B) Here as elsewhere, Rist appropriates contemporary culture for the purposes of re-evaluation and critique.
C) Frustration with songs that seem faddish has led some art critics to become frustrated with Rist's entire project.
D) Generally, Rist knows how to find the most beautiful aspects of mass-marketed entertainment.

9
A) NO CHANGE
B) Increasingly, the concept or idea behind the creation of artwork
C) Increasingly, the concept or idea behind the creation of artwork,
D) Increasingly, the concept or idea, behind the creation of artwork

10
A) NO CHANGE
B) had stood
C) has stood
D) stands

11
Which choice most effectively combines the sentences at the underlined portion?
A) although Rist records the creation of something emotional and visceral, rather than distantly ideological or academic, and makes art accessible to the viewer.
B) Rist records the creation of something emotional and visceral, rather than distantly ideological or academic, making art accessible to the viewer.
C) Rist records the creation of something emotional and visceral, rather than distantly ideological or academic in contrast to making art accessible to the viewer.
D) Rist records the creation of something emotional and visceral, rather than distantly ideological or academic; which makes art accessible to the viewer.

CONTINUE

Questions 12-22 are based on the following passage.

Lucky as an Owl

Owls, often associated with Athena, goddess of wisdom and war, can be regarded [12] to be totems of protection. It is said that the feather of an owl can repel illness and negative influences. In some countries, a dead owl nailed to a barn door is believed to [13] attract wild animals which spend the entire night staring at the figure. The silent passage of the owl through the forest night can be seen as a metaphor for the observation of ourselves by the gods, who make no comment but note all that we do (or do not do) in our passage through life. It is an unnerving metaphor perhaps, but also possibly a comforting one.

I am not the only one to believe this. The [14] Zuni, a Native American tribe, of the Pueblo peoples believe that placing an owl feather in a [15] babies crib guards the baby from evil spirits. Essentially, the hooting of an owl signifies the coming of death upon an individual. But [16] they left an owl feather in the crib was an attempt to confuse the owl so that death would not descend upon the infant. For me, it is unclear whether or not this custom indicates that the owl was truly a positive, benevolent force. Regardless, the prevalence of this practice means that, for the Zuni, the owl was benign.

I remember coming home after school to my Grandmother's house and [17] to see a large stuffed owl suspended from twine and attached to the frame of the front door. I am not really the superstitious type. I do not believe that adorning my car with a trinket of Saint Christopher will safeguard me from accidents or

12
A) NO CHANGE
B) as
C) like
D) for

13
Which choice best supports the point made about owls in the previous sentence?
A) NO CHANGE
B) bring wealth and fortune to a family.
C) ward off both wolves and robbers.
D) signify reverence for the power of large birds.

14
A) NO CHANGE
B) Zuni a Native American tribe of the Pueblo peoples,
C) Zuni—a Native American tribe of the Pueblo peoples,
D) Zuni, a Native American tribe of the Pueblo peoples,

15
A) NO CHANGE
B) babies'
C) babys'
D) baby's

16
A) NO CHANGE
B) if they had left
C) leaving
D) when they leave

17
A) NO CHANGE
B) I saw
C) I see
D) seeing

that [18] driving a car is ever really a safe activity. [19] Therefore, when I used to walk under her door, I felt all of my troubles melt away like snow. I felt invincible, protected, safe. Perhaps this feeling can really be explained by the comforts that Grandma had to offer [20] me: a warm snack, afternoon cartoons, and her little quips and anecdotes about her life in bucolic Tuscany. "Owls are good luck, dear. They keep the wolves away from the sheep. Just look at the eyes. Like daggers into a dark spirit's soul. No malicious force would dare cross an owl." Grandma would "hoot" at the owl any time she felt as though she were being watched. That strange yet familiar feeling of discomfort, which signified an intangible though unwelcome presence in the room, successfully faded with each "hoot."

Grandma passed away thirty years ago; since then, I [21] had kept my own version of her owl hanging wherever I have lived, from my childhood bedroom to my dorm room to [22] it's current resting place, my own home. Sometimes I "hoot" at the owl, remembering her. You may smile in a patronizing fashion at this, but my Grandma's old habit has worked so far.

18

Which choice offers a second supporting example that is most similar to the example earlier in the sentence?
A) NO CHANGE
B) a rabbit's foot is lucky.
C) birds of prey are typically malicious.
D) knocking on wood to avoid bad luck is ineffective.

19

A) NO CHANGE
B) In light of this,
C) Nonetheless,
D) Likewise,

20

A) NO CHANGE
B) me, a warm snack, afternoon cartoons, and,
C) me: a warm snack, afternoon, cartoons, and
D) me—a warm snack, afternoon cartoons, and,

21

A) NO CHANGE
B) have kept
C) will keep
D) would keep

22

A) NO CHANGE
B) its'
C) its
D) their

CONTINUE

Questions 23-33 are based on the following passage.

Earth Invades Mars!

The process of terraforming, or planetary engineering, was first proposed by science fiction writer Will Stuart in the [23] year 1940's, but has since been adopted as practical theory among modern scientists. Leading this group, Carl Sagan advocated the idea of terraforming Venus in *Science* journal (1961) and [24] later Mars in *Icarus* journal (1973). The process itself involves scientifically altering the environment of another planet to make it suitable for human habitation and biological growth, [25] without the use of elaborate life support systems. The practice is presently hypothetical and depends on a wide range of factors, including the current and historical geology, atmosphere, and chemical composition of the world in focus.

[1] These factors make certain planets appear better candidates for modification [26] than others. [2] Data from robot-operated spacecraft [27] has allowed scientists to determine that Mars was previously much more temperate and moist than its existing cold, dry climate would suggest. [3] By introducing certain greenhouse gases with low freezing points, planetary engineers would endeavor to thicken the existing atmosphere of Mars. [4] As a result, the surface might become sufficiently warm to once again generate liquid water and, eventually, to sustain biological ecosystems. [5] [28] At one point, liquid water flowed across the surface of the planet, forming the great canyons and mountains observable today.

23

A) NO CHANGE
B) 1940's
C) 1940 years
D) year and decade 1940

24

A) NO CHANGE
B) then later transforming Mars for
C) later Mars's transformation for
D) later doing Mars in

25

The writer is considering deleting the underlined sentence. Should the writer do this?

A) Yes, because science fiction novels seldom feature realistic life support systems.
B) Yes, because it simply re-phrases an idea presented slightly earlier.
C) No, because it gives a pertinent detail that clarifies the concept of terraforming.
D) No, because it highlights a limitation of past terraforming projects.

26

A) NO CHANGE
B) than it does others.
C) than others used to be.
D) than others are feasible to modify.

27

A) NO CHANGE
B) had
C) have
D) will have

28

To make this paragraph most logical, sentence 5 should be placed

A) where it is now.
B) after sentences 1.
C) after sentence 2.
D) after sentence 3.

Among the greenhouse gases with the potential for powerful heating effects are chlorofluorocarbons (or CFCs), which are human-generated organic compounds consisting of carbon, chlorine, and fluorine. Manufacturers have chiefly used these substances in refrigerants and aerosol products. In the late 1970's, scientists began arguing that such compounds [29] has significantly depleted the Earth's ozone layer; production of CFCs has since been heavily regulated. These compounds, so devastating to Earth's atmosphere, may be a paradoxical part of the recipe for transforming Mars into a Garden of Eden. The desired warming effect has already been marginally produced on Earth, and crudely demonstrates that humans are [30] capable about altering the climate on a planetary scale.

The initial goal of introducing greenhouse gases into the Martian atmosphere [31] is raising the mean temperature of the planet above the freezing point of water. Other stages of terraforming might involve the introduction of microbes to the Martian surface. These small organisms, while too tiny to see with the naked eye, produce many of the Earth's gases; some microbes do not need oxygen to survive. With very little liquid water, vast communities of microbes might subsist on the Martian soil. Through such soil consumption, these microscopic organisms [32] would expel quantities of gases large enough to help further insulate the planet. [33] Thus water would flow profusely, in a manner very similar to its origin on Earth.

29
A) NO CHANGE
B) had
C) were
D) will be

30
A) NO CHANGE
B) capable to alter
C) a capability to alter
D) capable of altering

31
A) NO CHANGE
B) is razing
C) is to raise
D) are raising

32
A) NO CHANGE
B) have expelled
C) do expel
D) expel

33
Which choice best supports the statement made in the previous sentence?
A) NO CHANGE
B) We could then study these organisms for clues to survival in extreme environments,
C) Thus life would begin on Mars,
D) The gas would cease to be harmful,

CONTINUE

Questions 34-44 are based on the following passage and supplementary material.

Mystery Shoppers: Commerce Goes Undercover

For some people, shopping is a tedious [34] chore, for others, it may be a source of enjoyment. For a third group, shopping is actually a job. The incognito business tactic known as "mystery shopping" has become an increasingly popular method of assessing customer satisfaction. While winning new customers is important, most business models stress the importance [35] in making sure of customer loyalty through repeated positive interactions; mystery shopping can help a business to gauge how consistently those positive interactions are taking place.

34

A) NO CHANGE
B) chore, which for
C) chore; but for
D) chore; for

35

A) NO CHANGE
B) of ensuring
C) in reassuring
D) of insuring

[1] Individuals who work as mystery shoppers function a bit like undercover detectives: by posing as people [36] who buy a product or using a service for personal purposes, these stealthy consumers are able to simulate a typical customer service interaction. [2] Mystery shoppers can be hired [37] providing assessments of customer service, vendor expertise, or product placement and display. [3] After this interaction, they will then provide a report either to the specific business or to a third-party customer assessment firm. [4] Depending on what aspect is under assessment, a mystery shopper may be given a specific task. [5] For example, someone hired to assess staff knowledge about a digital camera brand may be given a series of questions to ask and then be required to score how effectively the staff answered each inquiry. [6] Mystery shoppers need to be keenly observant, as small details are often [38] crucial, a shopper for instance, may be required to note an employee's manner of greeting customers or the position of an employee's name badge. [39]

[36]
A) NO CHANGE
B) buying a product or to use
C) buying a product or using
D) buy a product or use

[37]
A) NO CHANGE
B) provide
C) in providing
D) to provide

[38]
A) NO CHANGE
B) crucial: a shopper
C) crucial: a shopper,
D) crucial, a shopper,

[39]
To make this paragraph most logical, sentence 3 should be placed
A) where it is now.
B) after sentence 1.
C) after sentence 4.
D) after sentence 6.

CONTINUE

The mystery shopping industry has experienced steady growth in recent years, **40** although customer surveys are still the most popular form of customer service quality control. According to Fred Philips, the head of the store observation department for a major mystery shopping **41** firm; todays purchasers "have more disposable income and they want more service. They're not so price conscious, but they're more service

40

Which choice most effectively sets up the information in the following sentence?
A) NO CHANGE
B) yet research suggests that it will grow even more.
C) due largely to worsening customer service practices.
D) thanks in part to increasingly exacting customer service standards.

41

A) NO CHANGE
B) firm; today's
C) firm, todays
D) firm, today's

Mystery Shoppers

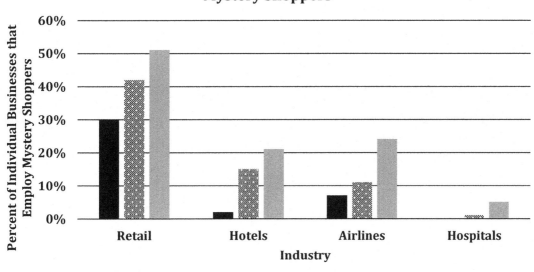

■ 2010 ※ 2011 ▨ 2012

conscious." There **42** <u>has also been</u> a steady expansion of mystery shopping practices outside of the retail industry. While hotels and airlines **43** <u>employ identical numbers of mystery shoppers, hospitals use mystery shoppers significantly less often.</u>

Many of the problems detected by mystery shoppers can be traced **44** <u>on</u> deficient employee knowledge and poor training. Mystery shoppers, indeed, are instrumental in pointing the way to specific enhancements. For some mystery shoppers, contributing to improved standards of customer service provides job satisfaction. An anonymous shopper who has worked in the industry for nearly ten years explains that he is motivated "to assist in providing a better shopping experience." For others, the thrill of maintaining secrecy can make working as a mystery shopper an interesting job.

42

A) NO CHANGE
B) were also
C) have also been
D) having also been

43

Which choice offers an accurate interpretation of the data in the chart?

A) NO CHANGE
B) have steadily increased in use of mystery shoppers, hospitals have also begun to employ mystery shoppers.
C) are not using mystery shoppers as much as hospitals, they use mystery shoppers much more than retail businesses.
D) have seen a recent downtrend in mystery shopper use, they are still using mystery shoppers more than hospitals.

44

A) NO CHANGE
B) to
C) for
D) in

STOP

If you finish before time is called, you may check your work on this section only.
Do not turn to any other section.

No Test Material On This Page

Answer Key: TEST 1

Test 1

READING: SECTION 1

PASSAGE 1	PASSAGE 2	PASSAGE 3	PASSAGE 4	PASSAGE 5
Fiction	Social Science	Natural Science 1	Global Conversation	Natural Science 2
1. C	11. C	21. A	31 A	42. A
2. B	12. C	22. D	32. D	43. C
3. C	13. B	23. D	33. D	44. B
4. B	14. A	24. A	34. C	45. D
5. C	15. C	25. B	35. B	46. A
6. A	16. C	26. B	36. B	47. B
7. A	17. B	27. C	37. A	48. B
8. C	18. A	28. A	38. D	49. A
9. C	19. B	29. C	39. C	50. B
10. C	20. C	30. B	40. D	51. C
			41. A	52. A

GRAMMAR: SECTION 2

PASSAGE 1	PASSAGE 2	PASSAGE 3	PASSAGE 4
The Gist of Pipilotti Rist	Lucky as an Owl	Earth Invades Mars!	Mystery Shoppers: Commerce Goes Undercover
1. B	12. B	23. B	34. D
2. C	13. C	24. A	35. B
3. B	14. D	25. C	36. C
4. B	15. D	26. A	37. D
5. A	16. C	27. C	38. C
6. D	17. D	28. C	39. B
7. D	18. B	29. B	40. D
8. B	19. C	30. D	41. D
9. B	20. A	31. C	42. A
10. D	21. B	32. A	43. B
11. B	22. C	33. C	44. B

Once you have determined how many questions
you answered correctly, consult the chart on Page 156
to determine **your scaled SAT Verbal score.**

Please visit **ies2400.com/answers** for answer explanations.

Post-Test Analysis

This post-test analysis is essential if you want to see an improvement on your next test. Possible reasons for errors on the Reading and Grammar passages in this test are listed here. Place check marks next to the types of errors that pertain to you, or write your own types of errors in the blank spaces.

TIMING AND ACCURACY

◇ Spent too long reading individual passages
◇ Spent too long answering each question
◇ Spent too long on a few difficult questions
◇ Felt rushed and made silly mistakes or random errors
◇ Unable to work quickly using error types and POE
Other: _____

APPROACHING THE PASSAGES AND QUESTIONS

◇ Unable to effectively grasp a passage's tone or style
◇ Unable to effectively grasp a passage's topic or stance
◇ Did not understand the context of line references or underlined portions
◇ Did not eliminate false answers using strong evidence
◇ Answered questions using first impressions instead of POE
◇ Answered questions without checking or inserting final answer
◇ Eliminated correct answer during POE
Other: _____

> **Use this form** to better analyze your performance. If you don't understand why you made errors, there is no way that you can correct them!

READING TEST: # CORRECT_____   # WRONG _____   # OMITTED _____

◇ Interpreted passages rather than working with evidence
◇ Used outside knowledge rather than working with evidence
◇ Unable to effectively identify a passage's purpose or argument
◇ Unable to work effectively with word in context questions
◇ Unable to work effectively with questions about structure and writing technique
◇ Unable to work accurately or efficiently with Command of Evidence questions
◇ Unable to draw logical conclusions based on the content of the passages
◇ Difficulties understanding graphics and relating them to the passages
Other: _____

GRAMMAR TEST: # CORRECT_____   # WRONG _____   # OMITTED _____

◇ Did not identify proper verb number, form, or tense
◇ Did identify proper pronoun agreement or pronoun form (subject/object, who/which/where)
◇ Did not test for proper comparison phrasing (amount/number, between/among)
◇ Did not test phrase for correct adverb/adjective usage
◇ Did not see broader sentence structure (parallelism, misplaced modifier)
◇ Did not see flaws in punctuation (colon, semicolon, comma splice, misplaced commas)
◇ Did not see tricky possessives or contractions (its/it's, your/you're)
◇ Did not identify flaws in standard phrases (either . . . or, not only . . . but also, etc.)
◇ Did not use proper phrasing in sentences requiring the subjunctive
◇ Did not notice wordiness, redundancy, or faulty idioms
◇ Did not notice excessively informal expressions or flaws in essay style
◇ Created the wrong relationship between two sentences or two paragraphs
◇ Created the wrong placement for an out-of-order paragraph
◇ Did not properly read or analyze an insertion/deletion question
◇ Did not properly read or analyze the information in a graphic
◇ Understood a graphic, but could not identify the correct passage content
Other: _____

Test 2

Reading Test
65 MINUTES, 52 QUESTIONS

Turn to Section 1 of your answer sheet to answer the questions in this section.

Each passage or pair of passages below is followed by a number of questions. After reading each passage or pair, choose the best answer to each question based on what is stated or implied in the passage or passages and in any accompanying graphics (such as a table or graph).

Questions 1-10 are based on the following passage.

This passage is adapted from a 2013 short story about a Midwestern man named Jermaine Wright, who has left his small town in Wisconsin to move to Boston, Massachusetts.

This was a new coffee shop. It was actually an old coffee shop, one of the oldest in America, first opened in 1874. But to Jermaine, it was a new coffee shop. Everything was new to
Line Jermaine. The Northeast ran at a different speed than Jermaine
5 did, but he found himself able to catch up, to run past the lazy ambling of his native Wisconsin. This was a new coffee shop, and he was a new Jermaine.

He didn't even necessarily want to leave Wisconsin, but his therapist thought it would be a good exercise in independence
10 and confronting his fears to move somewhere new, somewhere farther along. Frankly, Jermaine thought his therapist wanted a break from their sessions, and had even heard the therapist say something of the sort to his receptionist, but Jermaine told himself that his old paranoid fears of worthlessness were just
15 dogging him. Regardless of the reason for his new shift in location, Jermaine still called his therapist weekly, sometimes biweekly, to which his therapist would reply, "Hello Jermaine, what's the crisis this time?"

Jermaine sat down with his coffee, a large-sugar-no-
20 Splenda-soy-milk-no-dairy-hazelnut-and-as-little-froth-as-possible-brew, and thought about his new roommate. Jeff was an odd fellow, a little too happy and a little too friendly for Jermaine, but Jermaine supposed the situation could be worse. Jermaine Wright and Jeff Wozniak. "Double JW!" Jeff said. "JW
25 squared!" Jeff laughed. Jeff seemed to construe himself as a comedian, but Jermaine couldn't manage to find him funny. He simply smiled and waited for it all to be over.

What's worse were Jeff's cleaning habits. Jeff would leave his clothing strewn all about the apartment. Jermaine was rather
30 strict about tidiness, but only once had he found the courage to confront Jeff about it, a situation resulting in Jeff's comment, "Oh yeah, thank goodness we no longer live with our mothers!" Jermaine answered with a weak smile, and then a sigh, and he didn't bring up the topic again. He did begin to clean the
35 apartment, a development to which Jeff adjusted immediately.

Jermaine sipped his coffee, and pulled his laptop from his bag. He'd done enough thinking about Jeff for the day, he told himself. He pulled up the document he was working on; he was a freelancer, often picking up government projects, but he'd been
40 having problems lately. The websites and his friends had all said it was so easy to change your address, but Jermaine was having a hard time finding all the authorities he had to inform of the change. An immeasurable amount of work, yet it was supposedly no work at all. He would eventually get to it, but who could
45 stomach a day in line at the motor vehicle agency?

When all was said and done, Jermaine missed his native Wisconsin. When he remembered his time there, he remembered his old life with a tender pain, as he might remember an old friend who had moved away long ago. He thought of his
50 coworkers—here was the pain, with none of the tenderness—and he thought of his neighbors. He thought of his family—oh, his mother never quite let him be, maybe she was the one thing he was truly glad to be rid of. But he remembered fondly the way Ontario Drive swooped around in curves and buckled under
55 bridges. He missed the flat plains, and the way you could see a hundred trees stretched out over what felt like a hundred miles, and the way a snow drift could create a monument in just one night.

He couldn't say he hated the Northeast, though he could say
60 that Boston was not nearly as comfortable as Wisconsin was. He couldn't say Boston was less enjoyable, but he could say that it

CONTINUE ➡

was more stressful. He didn't feel as lost as he thought he would, though. He didn't feel as helpless as he thought he would. He had come here to get a break from the everyday particulars, and
65 he was certainly finding that, but with an important caveat: all days are the same in some sense.

1

The main purpose of this passage is to

A) catalog the differences between New England and the Midwest.

B) describe one man's inability to adapt to his new home.

C) portray the personality of an eccentric individual as he adjusts to a new location.

D) record the problems often encountered by roommates struggling to adapt to each other's idiosyncrasies.

2

It can be inferred that Jermaine views his move to New England as

A) less disorienting than he imagined.

B) impossible to accept.

C) temporary because of changing job opportunities.

D) agonizing because Jermaine misses his family.

3

Which choice provides the best evidence for the answer to the previous question?

A) Lines 8-11 ("He didn't . . . along")

B) Lines 33-35 ("Jermaine answered . . . immediately")

C) Lines 46-51 ("When all . . . neighbors")

D) Lines 62-63 ("He didn't . . . though")

4

Jermaine's therapist answers the phone in the manner he does in lines 17-18 ("Hello Jermaine . . . time") most likely because

A) the therapist suspects that the move was a bad idea for someone as sensitive as Jermaine and fears the worst.

B) the therapist is an old friend of Jermaine's family and is accustomed to the ups and downs of his relationship with Jermaine.

C) Jermaine's frequent complaints have led the therapist to expect a set pattern of behavior.

D) the therapist hopes that he and Jermaine will grow even closer if Jermaine returns.

5

Which of the following appears to provide Jermaine with the most stress?

A) Mundane details

B) Existential anxieties

C) Separation from his mother

D) Financial insecurities

6

As used in line 25, "construe" most nearly means

A) analyze.

B) reinvent.

C) present.

D) argue for.

7

As described in the third paragraph (lines 19-27), Jermaine's relationship with his roommate Jeff can best be characterized as

A) awkward but endurable.

B) hostile and contemptuous.

C) manipulative and unstable.

D) competitive but rewarding.

8

As used in line 45, "stomach" most nearly means

A) relish.

B) digest.

C) consume.

D) tolerate.

9

One of the primary problems that Jermaine faces is

A) anger management.

B) emotional dependence.

C) absentmindedness.

D) low self-confidence.

10

Which choice provides the best evidence for the answer to the previous question?

A) Lines 4-7 ("The Northeast . . . Jermaine")

B) Lines 13-15 ("but Jermaine . . . him")

C) Lines 43-45 ("An immeasurable . . . agency?")

D) Lines 55-58 ("He missed . . . night")

CONTINUE ➤ **45**

Questions 11-21 are based on the following passage and supplementary material.

In the following passage, the author discusses the "slavery footprint" of every individual and how we can work to reduce global slavery.

Consumerism is on the rise: we want more, we want it fast, and we want it cheap. Our landfills are growing as we accumulate and quickly disregard more and more possessions.
Line So it shouldn't come as a shock to know that our carbon footprint
5 is getting larger. But most people are unaware that our slavery footprint is expanding as well. This happens whenever we buy products that in some way support modern slavery. If you own a computer, a decent number of shoes, or a bike of just about any sort, you probably have somewhere in the neighborhood of 100
10 slaves working for you.

A recently launched website called slaveryfootprint.org, which is backed by the U.S. State Department, defines a slave as "anyone who is forced to work without pay, is being economically exploited, and is unable to walk away." Through
15 this site, we can calculate how connected to human trafficking and slave labor we are. Knowing that we might have a hand in perpetuating such evils, we should at least take a moment to think about the consequences of our role in consumer society.

The site offers a survey that, when completed, determines
20 the exact slavery footprint of any given visitor. Participants in the survey feed in information about their lifestyles and purchasing trends, and a sophisticated algorithm calculates where geographically their possessions were made. After that, the site searches its database to estimate the prevalence of slavery
25 in these areas and produces a number representing the slavery footprint. The results are staggering. The average person has about 27 slaves working for him or her, and half of those slaves are active at any given moment. This means that the majority of the products we use on a daily basis has at some point passed
30 through the hands of a slave.

With roughly 30 million slaves in the world today, chances are that most of what we buy has at one time or another come into contact with a slave. Chocolate, though processed and packaged by fancy European boutiques, is made from cocoa
35 beans which are gathered by the small hands of slave children across West Africa. Leather from India is often obtained through the forced labor of lower-caste workers. The Thai seafood industry relies on the labor of Cambodian, Burmese, and Malaysian slaves. Coltan, a superconductor used in electronics
40 such as cell phones, is mined by slaves in the Democratic Republic of the Congo. Even in the cosmetics industry, tens of thousands of Indian children mine mica, the little sparkles in makeup, and China's migrant population often produces the silica in nail polish. And these are only a few of the products we
45 come across daily that depend on slave labor.

This does not mean that all the companies we patronize endorse slave labor, or knowingly run sweatshops. Nor does it necessarily mean that we should vilify a company upon finding out that it is somehow connected to slave labor. What we need
50 to do is understand the supply chains at the heart of the problem; most companies rely on other companies for processed and raw materials, unaware sometimes of where these materials originate. We as consumers have the obligation to do the research, and it is incumbent on us, as the end-users of these products, to bring
55 modern slavery to the attention of influential companies. Only if we can rally together and do this in a large way can we have a shot at combating slavery.

On the Slavery Footprint website, users can download the "Free World" software and use it to research brands and
60 stores. Users can also send letters to various companies, requesting inquiries into their supply chains. Companies that receive these letters, fearing negative press about their links to slavery, are more likely to check whether or not their suppliers are in fact utilizing slave labor. Nothing mobilizes
65 business more than the threat of a public relations fiasco. But steps toward a solution can't start until consumers become more aware of the problem.

For most people, slavery is something that happens in distant places, or only happened long ago. But slaveryfootprint.
70 org brings this affliction to our doorstep, and reminds us that by staying unaware and inactive, we are complicit in slavery today.

CONTINUE

Human Trafficking Victims and Legislation

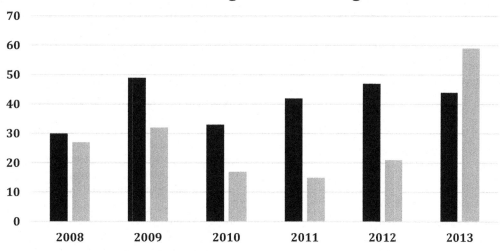

■ Identified Victims (Thousands)   ▨ New or Amended Legislation

11

The primary purpose of the passage is to

A) remind readers that slavery still exists today in one continent.

B) introduce a website that can help to combat a problem.

C) argue that the electronics industry is solely responsible for slavery.

D) highlight certain industries that should be boycotted.

12

The main effect of the author's phrasing in lines 4-6 ("So it . . . as well") is to

A) illustrate the impact of human civilization on the natural landscape.

B) explain the connection between humanitarian struggles and the U.S. State Department.

C) use the language of a well-known problem to introduce a lesser-known one.

D) create an analogy between two seemingly disparate environmental concerns.

13

As used in line 15, "connected to" most nearly means

A) combined with.

B) tied to.

C) akin to.

D) aware of.

14

According to the author, what is responsible for increasing a slavery footprint?

A) Lowering trade restrictions

B) Creating overseas factories

C) Developing new technologies

D) Consuming products

15

Which choice provides the best evidence for the answer to the previous question?

A) Lines 6-7 ("This happens . . . slavery")

B) Lines 26-28 ("The average . . . moment")

C) Lines 46-47 ("This does . . . sweatshops")

D) Lines 49-52 ("What we . . . originate")

16

The author develops an argument in lines 31-45 by

A) demonstrating the widespread prevalence of slavery.

B) listing every national economy that depends on slavery.

C) suggesting a course of action that will combat slavery.

D) analyzing the productivity of slave-dependent nations.

17

Which of the following does the author suggest that the reader do?

A) Publicly criticize expensive brands

B) Investigate company suppliers

C) Avoid purchasing imported merchandise

D) Visit the U.S. State Department

18

Which choice provides the best evidence for the answer to the previous question?

A) Lines 14-16 ("Through . . . we are")

B) Lines 17-18 ("we should . . . society")

C) Lines 31-33 ("With roughly . . . a slave")

D) Lines 60-61 ("Users can . . . chains")

19

As used in line 61, "chains" most nearly means

A) cords.

B) confines.

C) bindings.

D) networks.

20

Do the data in the graph directly support the author's ideas about effective ways to combat slavery?

A) Yes, because the amount of legislation increased sharply between 2012 and 2014.

B) Yes, because the most victims were identified in 2009.

C) No, because the author never discusses slavery-related legislation.

D) No, because the number of identfied victims has not decreased significantly.

21

Which claim about human trafficking is supported by the graph?

A) The number of victims identified directly corresponds to the amount of new or amended legislation.

B) Both the highest number of victims identified and the highest amount of new or amended legislation were seen in 2013.

C) The lowest number of victims identified was recorded in 2011.

D) Both the number of victims identified and the amount of new or amended legislation were higher in 2013 than in 2008.

Questions 22-32 are based on the following passage and supplementary material.

Over the past decade, environmentalists and engineers have attempted to find new ways to deal with the scarcity of natural resources in central Africa. The author of this passage considers one new invention and its possible impact on society and ecology in Ethiopia.

The *Ficus vasta* or, to give its everyday name, the Warka tree is immense in size. Its massive trunk grows to a height of twenty-five meters and its branches spread to form an inverted
Line bowl that can reach fifty meters in width. As its Latin name
5 indicates, this mammoth plant is a member of the fig (*Ficus*) family; indeed, it produces a fruit which can be eaten by sheep, goats, baboons, monkeys, and children.

Typically, the Warka tree grows along the banks of rivers, though it can also be found in the savannas of Uganda and
10 Tanzania and in ecosystems well beyond these countries, particularly in the Horn of Africa. This plant has grown in the Sudan, in Somalia, and in Ethiopia. However, visitors to these nations would be hard-pressed to find any Warkas—or, in some regions, any trees of any kind. There was a time when this was
15 not the case, yet one of the consequences of the extreme poverty in these parts of the world has been deforestation. When trees are chopped down to provide wood for cooking fires, but cannot be replaced by local communities, the result is barren land where life of all sorts begins to die out. These African countries expose,
20 in a particularly stark manner, the consequences of the human struggle for basic survival.

Over seven million of the people who live in sub-Saharan Africa do not have regular access to water; these Africans rely on water holes that are often approximately fifty kilometers from
25 their homes and that can only be accessed on foot. Even in the areas of Ethiopia where there is water at hand, this water lies one thousand and fifty feet below tough, rocky terrain. To break through without heavy machinery is impossible. Even if such excavation could be achieved, there is little chance that the water
30 could be pumped to the surface without electrical power, which is also hard to come by in these regions. On account of such scarcities, solutions that are at once minimal and ingenious are necessary.

One promising proposal for these troubled regions of
35 Africa has come from Arturo Vittori, an Italian artist, architect, and industrial designer. Vittori has designed subways, yachts, and the largest existing airliner, the A380. He has even created prototypes for an extreme environment tent and for a pressurized rover that humans could use to drive across Mars. Most recently,
40 he traveled to Ethiopia and witnessed the devastating problems caused by the lack of available water. He also saw, for the first time in his life, a magnificent *Ficus vasta*. Then he went home and designed the WarkaWater.

CONTINUE

In appearance, the WarkaWater mimics the tree that inspired
45 its design: a "trunk" eight meters high narrows at its top (just
like the neck of a bottle) before suddenly expanding to a width
of almost eight meters. Nobody has yet weighed an actual Warka
tree: this facsimile weighs, in total, sixty kilograms, and can be
created by four people with the aid of a simple cutting machine.
50 Bamboo strips are bound together in the shape of a Warka tree,
forming a pattern of crossed stalks. These stalks are then linked
by a mesh of nylon and polypropylene fibers. Thus, a scaffold for
condensation has been built: overnight, dew forms on the fibers
and rolls down the strands into a collecting basin at the base of
55 the structure. In this way, over one hundred liters of drinkable
water can be collected every day.

The whole construction is hand-crafted yet is based on the
same precision modeling that is used to create the interior of
an aircraft. The highly portable WarkaWater is both artistic and
60 practical: it links the needs of Ethiopia's nomadic communities
with the scientific ambitions of the twenty-first century. In a
sense, Vittori has shown that elements of traditional societies, far
from being hindrances to progress, can show us how to preserve
the earth we inhabit.

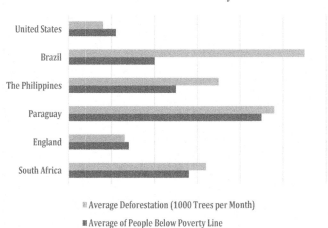

Deforestation and Poverty

- United States
- Brazil
- The Philippines
- Paraguay
- England
- South Africa

■ Average Deforestation (1000 Trees per Month)
■ Average of People Below Poverty Line

22

The passage suggests that deforestation is primarily a by-product of

A) a booming lumber industry.
B) changing weather conditions.
C) irresponsible farming methods.
D) widespread chronic poverty.

23

It can be inferred from the passage that Vittori designed the WarkaWater because

A) he saw the invention as a means of turning an enormous profit.
B) he wanted to re-create a natural marvel for aesthetic pleasure.
C) he wanted to alleviate suffering.
D) he needed a new architectural challenge.

24

Which choice provides the best evidence for the answer to the previous question?

A) Lines 36-37 ("Vittori . . . A380")
B) Lines 39-41 ("Most recently . . . water")
C) Lines 41-42 ("He also . . . *Ficus vasta*")
D) Lines 44-47 ("In appearance . . . meters")

25

The information in the third paragraph (lines 22-33) conveys the idea that the problem of water shortage in Africa is

A) trivial.
B) dramatic.
C) manageable.
D) localized.

26

As used in line 32, the word "minimal" most nearly means

A) low-profile.
B) negligible.
C) inexpensive.
D) insignificant.

27

The author includes a list of Vittori's achievements primarily in order to

A) underscore Vittori's ingenuity in solving engineering problems.
B) reinforce Vittori's growing reputation for creativity.
C) indicate the background needed to solve a humanitarian problem.
D) contrast Vittori's humble origins with his present-day renown.

CONTINUE   49

28

Which of the following statements is best supported by the passage?

A) The Warka tree grows abundantly throughout Africa.

B) Though native to many regions, the Warka tree is now rare.

C) The Warka tree is a significant source of nourishment.

D) The Warka tree resists cultivation.

29

Which choice provides the best evidence for the answer to the previous question?

A) Lines 4-7 ("As its . . . and children")

B) Lines 8-11 ("Typically . . . Africa")

C) Lines 11-14 ("This plant . . . kind")

D) Lines 16-19 ("When trees . . . die out")

30

As used in line 49, the word "created" most nearly means

A) conceived.

B) inspired.

C) designed.

D) produced.

31

Which of the following statements is most supported by the graph?

A) Average deforestation is always directly proportional to a country's average poverty level.

B) Average poverty level is determined directly by the average deforestation per month.

C) Average deforestation is inversely related to a country's poverty level.

D) The average poverty level of a country exists in independence of its monthly deforestation.

32

Based on information in the graphic and the passage, the relation between deforestation and poverty in Ethiopia is least similar to the situation in which country?

A) Brazil

B) The Philippines

C) Paraguay

D) South Africa

CONTINUE

Questions 33-42 are based on the following passage.

Originally published under the title "Docility and Dependence," this passage is one of the short essays that appears in *A Treatise on Parents and Children* by George Bernard Shaw (1856-1950).

If anyone, impressed by my view that the rights of a child
are precisely those of an adult, proceeds to treat a child as
if it were an adult, he (or she) will find that though the plan
Line will work much better at some points than the usual plan, at
5 others, it will not work at all; as it happens, this discovery
may provoke him to turn back from the whole conception of
children's rights with a jest at the expense of bachelors' and old
maids' children. In dealing with children what is needed is not
logic but sense. There is no logical reason why young persons
10 should be allowed greater control of their property the day after
they are twenty-one than the day before it. There is no logical
reason why I, who strongly object to an adult standing over a
boy of ten with a Latin grammar, and saying, "you must learn
this, whether you want to or not," should nevertheless be quite
15 prepared to stand over a boy of five with the multiplication
table or a copy book or a code of elementary good manners,
and practice on his docility to make him learn them. And there
is no logical reason why I should do for a child a great many
little offices, some of them troublesome and disagreeable,
20 which I should not do for a boy twice his age, or support a boy
or girl when I would unhesitatingly throw an adult on his own
resources. But there are practical reasons, and sensible reasons,
and affectionate reasons for all these illogicalities.
Children do not want to be treated altogether as adults:
25 such treatment terrifies them and over-burdens them with
responsibility. In truth, very few adults care to be called on
for independence and originality: they also are bewildered
and terrified in the absence of precedents and precepts and
commandments, but modern Democracy allows them a
30 sanctioning and canceling power if they are capable of using
it, which children are not. To treat a child wholly as an adult
would be to mock and destroy it. Infantile docility and juvenile
dependence are, like death, the products of Natural Selection;
and though there is no viler crime than to abuse them, yet there
35 is no greater cruelty than to ignore them. I have complained
sufficiently of what I suffered through the process of assault,
imprisonment, and compulsory lessons that taught me nothing,
which are called my schooling. But I could say a good deal
also about the things I was not taught and should have been
40 taught, not to mention the things I was allowed to do which I
should not have been allowed to do. I have no recollection of
being taught to read or write, so I presume I was born with both
faculties, but many people seem to have bitter recollections
of being forced reluctantly to acquire them. And though I
45 have the uttermost contempt for a teacher so ill mannered and

incompetent as to be unable to make a child learn to read and
write without also making it cry, still I am prepared to admit
that I had rather have been compelled to learn to read and write
with tears by an incompetent and ill mannered person than left
50 in ignorance. Reading, writing, and enough arithmetic to use
money honestly and accurately, together with the rudiments of
law and order, become necessary conditions of a child's liberty
before it can appreciate the importance of its liberty, or foresee
that these accomplishments are worth acquiring. Nature has
55 provided for this by evolving the instinct of docility. Children
are very docile: they have a sound intuition that they must
do what they are told or perish. And adults have an intuition,
equally sound, that they must take advantage of this docility
to teach children how to live properly or the children will not
60 survive. The difficulty is to know where to stop.

33

Bernard Shaw uses repetition in lines 9-22 ("There is . . .
resources") in order to

A) suggest that the way adults treat children should be
more logical.

B) indicate that he disagrees with traditional modes of
education.

C) imply that he finds children disagreeable.

D) emphasize that sensible actions are not always logical.

34

It can most reasonably be inferred that Bernard Shaw
believes that children

A) have the same rights as adults and should be treated as
such.

B) will naturally acquire the ability to read and write.

C) cannot yet appreciate the importance of education.

D) enjoy learning with their peers more than learning with
adults.

35

Bernard Shaw implies that his education was

A) neither fruitful nor comprehensive.

B) essential to his writing career.

C) similar to that granted to most children.

D) guided by illogical procedures.

36

According to the author, the "difficulty" (line 60) that adults face is knowing when to stop

A) exercising control over children.

B) teaching basic skills to children.

C) believing that children have rights.

D) treating children like adults.

37

According to the passage, adults are able to compel children to learn because

A) adults have more power in a democracy.

B) children are naturally obedient.

C) adults treat children as their equals.

D) children depend on adults for sustenance.

38

Which choice provides the best evidence for the answer to the previous question?

A) Lines 3-5 ("he . . . at all")

B) Lines 38-40 ("But I . . . taught")

C) Lines 47-50 ("still I . . . ignorance")

D) Lines 54-56 ("Nature . . . docile")

39

According to the passage, adults are similar to children because they

A) feel uncertain without guidance.

B) enjoy sanctioning and canceling powers.

C) can survive without relying on others.

D) dislike persons of higher authority.

40

Which choice provides the best evidence for the answer to the previous question?

A) Lines 5-8 ("as it . . . maids' children")

B) Lines 27-29 ("they also . . . commandments")

C) Lines 31-32 ("To treat . . . it")

D) Lines 43-44 ("but many . . . them")

41

As used in line 2, "proceeds" most nearly means

A) approaches.

B) undertakes.

C) advances.

D) evolves.

42

As used in line 56, "sound" most nearly means

A) universal.

B) valid.

C) tested.

D) tangible.

CONTINUE

Questions 43-52 are based on the following passages.

In these passages, two authors consider how food shortages relate to concepts from plant biology.

Passage 1

The cultivated peanuts of today have lost most of their former genetic resistance to disease; as a result, peanut plants have immense trouble reproducing, and peanut crops have nearly
Line been decimated. Imagine a world without jars of peanuts on
5 the shelves or peanut butter cups in vending machines—hard, right? The same goes for the banana: did you know that it is sterile? The yellow bunched fruit that can be found at the market is actually a genetically cloned mutant and cannot reproduce on its own. The wild type, which is capable of spreading seeds
10 (and seeds the size of capers), is neither as delectable nor as marketable as its barren counterpart. Because of their diminished immunities and nonexistent reproductive capabilities, these foods are at risk of disappearing from global commerce as increasingly robust pathogen populations threaten the futures of
15 peanut and banana crops.

The cases of the peanut and the banana are only two examples of how a lack of biological diversity can diminish a plant population necessary to a cash crop industry. Concern with plant inbreeding hearkens back to The Great Famine of 1845,
20 when the Potato Blight eradicated a staple of Irish nutrition; in the course of this crisis, mass starvation took the lives of nearly one million people over six years.

Indeed, the Potato Blight's cost in human life was staggering, but the loss of expertise and labor should not be
25 underestimated: almost 4.5 million Irish, the horrors of the potato blight ever in mind, left their home country between 1850 and 1921. Greater cross-breeding of potatoes would have facilitated genetic variation, would have fostered more robust strains, and might have prevented a nationwide catastrophe. Sadly for those
30 remaining in Ireland, some of the agricultural talent needed for cross-breeding had been eradicated, or driven out of the country, by the Potato Blight itself.

Passage 2

For some, hardships pave the way for ingenuity. Even in nations that have been afflicted by food shortages, it is possible
35 to push back against the worst economic and agricultural pressures. Nikolai Vavilov (1887-1943), who eventually became one of Russia's most prominent geneticists and botanists, grew up in an era when hunger was omnipresent and food was scarce. Determined to create a better existence for his family and for
40 mankind as a whole, Vavilov dedicated his life to comprehending the root of starvation and to developing the means of preventing food crises. To consolidate his work on these problems, he collected agricultural seeds from five continents and established a seed bank.

45 Vavilov's seed bank was instrumental in promoting genetic classification and preservation as a truly modern system of scientific inquiry—and of humanitarian involvement. Because orthodox seeds (those that can survive drying or freezing, and that are suited to remote conservation) can remain in a dormant
50 state for decades with properly controlled temperature and humidity conditions, their DNA will sustain little damage and the seed itself can remain viable, functioning almost as an organic time capsule. It is possible to compare this famous seed bank to the civilization-saving storehold of Noah's Ark; Vavilov,
55 certainly, was interested in protecting civilization, not with paired-off animals but with the plant strains that would ensure a healthy future.

43

In discussing the science of seeds, the author of Passage 1 and the author of Passage 2 both present

A) specific historical examples.

B) profiles of famous scientists.

C) cutting-edge technological solutions.

D) literary and religious references.

44

As used in line 1, "cultivated" most nearly means

A) modified.

B) proliferating.

C) refined.

D) cultured.

45

The examples of "Greater cross breeding" (Passage 1, line 27) and "orthodox seeds" (Passage 2, line 48) would best support the idea that

A) research must be undertaken to counteract starvation.

B) agricultural scientists can foster especially durable plants.

C) the Potato Blight involved genetically manipulated seeds.

D) agriculture based on inbred strains of seeds will ultimately fail.

46

The primary purpose of Passage 2 is to

A) illustrate the variety of seeds available to counteract hunger.

B) directly contradict the ideas put forward in Passage 1.

C) show how an early life filled with hardship can lead a scientist to success.

D) discuss the significance of work that addressed a specific humanitarian problem.

47

Which choice provides the best evidence for the answer to the previous question?

A) Lines 36-38 ("Nikolai . . . scarce")

B) Lines 42-44 ("To consolidate . . . seed bank")

C) Lines 47-53 ("Because . . . capsule")

D) Lines 53-54 ("It is possible . . . Noah's Ark")

48

If Nikolai Vavilov's development of "orthodox seeds" had taken place by 1845, the discovery would most likely have had what effect on the scenario described in Passage 1?

A) One million Irish deaths would have happened over ten years instead of over six years.

B) Genetic variation would have allowed fruit and nut crops to remedy Ireland's potato shortage.

C) Ireland might not have lost so many great minds and diligent workers to the Potato Blight.

D) Some of the world's greatest agricultural talent would never have been discovered.

49

The author of Passage 1 would most likely regard Vavilov's findings as discussed in Passage 2 as

A) enlightening, since the findings prove that genetic uniformity tends to weaken plant species over time.

B) questionable, since none of Vavilov's ideas have been experimentally validated.

C) limited, because Vavilov had little interest in the psychological effects of famine.

D) valuable, because disasters can result from poor knowledge of the best agricultural practices.

50

Which choice provides the best evidence for the answer to the previous question?

A) Lines 1-4 ("The . . . decimated")

B) Lines 23-25 ("Indeed . . . underestimated")

C) Lines 27-29 ("Greater . . . catastrophe")

D) Lines 29-32 ("Sadly . . . eradicated")

51

As used in line 9, "wild" most nearly means

A) original.

B) unruly.

C) energized.

D) unregulated.

52

Passage 1 and Passage 2 examine the topic of seed biology in a manner best described as

A) hypothetical and experimental.

B) factual yet counterintuitive.

C) anecdotal and scientific.

D) informal and accessible.

STOP

If you finish before time is called, you may check your work on this section only.
Do not turn to any other section.

No Test Material On This Page

Writing Test
35 MINUTES, 44 QUESTIONS

Turn to Section 2 of your answer sheet to answer the questions in this section.

DIRECTIONS

Each passage below is accompanied by a number of questions. For some questions, you will consider how the passage might be revised to improve the expression of ideas. For other questions, you will consider how the passage might be edited to correct errors in sentence structure, usage, or punctuation. A passage or a question may be accompanied by one or more graphics (such as a table or graph) that you will consider as you make revising and editing decisions.

Some questions will direct you to an underlined portion of a passage. Other questions will direct you to a location in a passage or ask you to think about the passage as a whole.

After reading each passage, choose the answer to each question that most effectively improves the quality of writing in the passage or that makes the passage conform to the conventions of standard written English. Many questions include a "NO CHANGE" option. Choose that option if you think the best choice is to leave the relevant portion of the passage as it is.

Questions 1-11 are based on the following passage.

Keeping Your Cool with Hot-Desking

"Hot-desking" refers to a system of workplace organization in which different individuals utilize the same workspace (either a desk or a physical office) on a rotating basis. This contrasts with traditional systems of organization in which workers are assigned permanent spaces, often according to status or seniority. Technology, particularly a reliance on mobile devices, make it possible for employees to move more easily between different workspaces and has facilitated the rise of hot-desking. Desires for more flexible working hours, as well as the option to work from home or from another remote location, can be much more readily accommodated within a hot-desk workplace.

A) NO CHANGE
B) made
C) have made
D) has made

CONTINUE

[2] Hot-desking, offers a number of advantages, which businesses often cite when deciding whether to adopt this model. It accounts for the reality of a high proportion of workers not being physically present in the office at [3] once, according to a study conducted in 2013, approximately 30% of the individual offices in American workplaces are vacant at any given time. Employee vacancies may be due to travel, meetings (both in conference rooms and off-site), or decisions to work from home. Hot-desking therefore allows businesses to maintain spaces that are proportional to the number of individuals likely to be occupying a given office at the same time, rather than [4] about the total number of employees. The option to lease a smaller space then becomes a possibility, and this possibility is especially attractive in major city centers, [5] where rent can become a significant operational cost.

2
A) NO CHANGE
B) Hot-desking:
C) Hot-desking
D) Hot-desking—

3
A) NO CHANGE
B) once; according
C) once—according
D) once, so according

4
A) NO CHANGE
B) with
C) on
D) to

5
A) NO CHANGE
B) which
C) when
D) that

[6] Despite the economic benefits for employers, there may be other advantages to hot-desking. This method of office organization both makes it easier for employees to work remotely [7] while creating an office culture that encourages this practice. It may also boost creativity and collaboration, and encourage greater levels of interaction between employees with different jobs. [8] But there are drawbacks to hot-desking.

6

Which choice best connects the sentence with the previous paragraph?

A) NO CHANGE
B) In addition to economic benefits for employers,
C) Besides the savings for employees,
D) Though operational costs vary from city to city,

7

A) NO CHANGE
B) while it creates
C) and creates
D) and creating

8

The writer is considering deleting the underlined sentence. Should the writer do this?

A) Yes, because it detracts from the writer's main point in this paragraph.
B) Yes, because it makes a claim about hot-desking that is not supported by the passage.
C) No, because it supports the passage's argument that hot-desking is ultimately detrimental.
D) No, because it illustrates a general principle discussed in this paragraph.

CONTINUE

[1] However, critics point out that many individuals tend to prefer the stability, routine, and sense of control associated with having an individualized, permanent workspace. [2] Workspace distribution in many offices has also often been traditionally tied to status within the organization. [3] If employees feel threatened or competitive due to unfamiliar workspace arrangements, **9** they're feelings can heighten interpersonal conflict, leading to disruptions and reduced efficiency. [4] By allowing employees to work in many different spaces, including spaces outside of the office, hot-desking **10** may possibly also make it more difficult for employers to monitor productivity. [5] For example, a promotion to a more senior role might be accompanied by a move to a larger or more desirable office. [6] Yet whether it is a benefit or a drawback, hot-desking, in many modern offices, is here to stay. **11**

9
A) NO CHANGE
B) their
C) his or her
D) there

10
A) NO CHANGE
B) may
C) might have
D) may perhaps

11
To make this paragraph most logical, sentence 5 should be placed
A) where it is now.
B) after sentence 1.
C) after sentence 2.
D) after sentence 3.

Questions 12-22 are based on the following passage.

Pantomime Time

It is quite difficult to explain to anyone who is not British what exactly Pantomime is. Foreigners are bemused by this particular theatrical genre, which [12] appears annually from Christmas to March every year. Clearly it is [13] popular, it plays to packed houses. Going to see a "Panto" at Christmas [14] have often been the first (and, in many cases, the only) time a child is ever taken to the theater. The whole family goes, for a holiday treat, so there has to be something about the show that will appeal to each member of the family. The theme always concerns a poor and good hero making his way to success and riches against all odds. An element of magic [15] could be important, since it allows for a "transformation" scene, which is always the dynamic, sparkling climax to the first half of the Pantomime. Children (and very often adults) sit agape when such a spectacle unfolds before their eyes.

12

A) NO CHANGE
B) every year appears from Christmas to March, annually.
C) annually appears from Christmas to March.
D) it appears annually from Christmas to March.

13

A) NO CHANGE
B) popular: it
C) popular when it
D) popular it

14

A) NO CHANGE
B) were often
C) was often being
D) has often been

15

A) NO CHANGE
B) would be
C) was
D) is

CONTINUE

[1] A proper "Panto" [16] is a thoroughly rehearsed performance: "something for everyone" necessitates the inclusion of acrobatics, dancing, music, and, above all, glamor and comedy. [2] [17] In other words, these two last elements are created through role reversal and cross dressing—techniques that may strike audiences beyond Britain as strange, but that are Pantomime essentials. [3] "He" is always played by a woman, who strides across the stage dressed as a man. [4] The comedy is provided by the character of the Dame, always played by a deep-voiced man in a big wig, billowy costume, and exaggerated makeup. [5] This role reversal is one of the ways in which the Pantomime takes on the surrealism of a dream and motivates the audience to suspend the logic of everyday life. [18]

[16]

Which choice best introduces the information that follows?
A) NO CHANGE
B) is an eclectic affair
C) performs nearly every night
D) carefully coordinates a sophisticated set of performers

[17]

A) NO CHANGE
B) However,
C) To avoid confusion,
D) DELETE the underlined portion and begin the sentence with a capital letter.

[18]

The writer plans to add the following sentence to this paragraph.

The Hero is the Pantomime character who imparts glamor to the whole show.

To make this paragraph most logical, the sentence should be placed
A) after sentence 1.
B) after sentence 2.
C) after sentence 3.
D) after sentence 4.

[19] The most extraordinary element of Pantomime is the participation of the audience. They are encouraged to sing along with the cast, call out when the hero is in danger, join in the moments of slapstick comedy on stage, boo the villain, and sigh contentedly when the hero finally wins the heroine. A tremendous sense of relationship builds up between the characters on the stage [20] to the real life of the audience: topical jokes, innuendos, and characters coming down from the stage and mixing with the audience are all favored "Panto" techniques. [21] The final moments of a Pantomime bring this interactive element to a climax. The Dame appears in front of the curtain and a huge sheet printed with song lyrics descends.

19

Which choice most effectively combines the underlined sentences?

A) The audience is encouraged to sing along with the cast, call out when the hero is in danger, join in the moments of slapstick comedy on stage, boo the villain, and sigh contentedly when the hero finally wins the heroine, this audience participation is the most extraordinary element of Pantomime.

B) The audience's participation, which is encouraged to sing along with the cast, call out when the hero is in danger, join in the moments of slapstick comedy on stage, boo the villain, and sigh contentedly when the hero finally wins the heroine, is the most extraordinary element of Pantomime.

C) The most extraordinary element of Pantomime is the participation of the audience, which is encouraged to sing along with the cast, call out when the hero is in danger, join in the moments of slapstick comedy on stage, boo the villain, and sigh contentedly when the hero finally wins the heroine.

D) The most extraordinary element of Pantomime, which is encouraged to sing along with the cast, call out when the hero is in danger, join in the moments of slapstick comedy on stage, boo the villain, and sigh contentedly when the hero finally wins the heroine, is the participation of the audience.

20

A) NO CHANGE
B) and
C) for
D) as

21

The writer is considering deleting the underlined sentence. Should the sentence be kept or deleted?

A) Kept, because it introduces and identifies the relevance of the following sentences.

B) Kept, because it points out that audience participation is only important in one part of the play.

C) Deleted, because it blurs the focus of the paragraph by shifting to a summary of the play's ending.

D) Deleted, because it weakens the writer's point about Pantomime being a cheerful genre.

CONTINUE

The Dame and the audience now work together one last time, chatting, interacting, and [22] they sing together lustily. Then, prompted by a drum roll, those onstage return to their seats. The Dame exits, and the curtains part to reveal the final scene, where the villains are thwarted and the hero and heroine are united, rich at last and greeted with the audience's happy applause.

22
A) NO CHANGE
B) sing
C) singing
D) they would sing

Questions 23-33 are based on the following passage.

Finding the Missing Lynx

[23] The lynx has roamed the earth for over two million years, and has wandered at times into human folklore. Throughout Europe and Northern America, there [24] have arose myths that emphasize the elusive and mysterious powers of this relatively small wildcat. Folk tales speak of an alliance between the lynx and the Morning Star: it was believed that the animal's remarkable powers of vision were linked with the purity of that star's light. From this association stemmed the belief that the animal's sight could pierce solid objects and reach what might be hidden from others. Indeed, the rugged independence of the lynx made it a figure of power, and its very isolation [25] (since these wildcats avoid human settlements) gave it an almost mystical status.

There are currently four distinct variations of lynx in the Northern hemisphere: Iberian, Eurasian, Canadian, and Bobcat. All species mate in late winter; cubs are born within two months and stay with their mothers for about a year before setting off on their own. The appearance of the typical lynx is both [26] elegant and practical. Its fur can range in color from gold to white. The lynx's ears are often tipped with black hair; its tail is short and its paws are padded for walking on snow. High-altitude forests and rocky heights, far from human habitation, [27] has long been the animal's natural habitat.

23

Which choice most effectively introduces the main idea of the paragraph?
A) NO CHANGE
B) The lynx is not only a beautiful creature but also a daunting and unusual one.
C) Through the ages, the human imagination has been drawn to elusive and ferocious animals.
D) Animal activists are in an uproar over declines in lynx populations.

24

A) NO CHANGE
B) were raised
C) have arisen
D) are arising

25

At this point, the writer is considering deleting the following portion of the sentence.

(since these wildcats avoid human settlements)

Should the writer make this deletion?
A) Yes, because it is redundant.
B) Yes, because it contradicts a previous statement.
C) No, because it clarifies the preceding statement.
D) No, because it mentions the impact of humans on the lynx.

26

Which choice most effectively combines the two sentences at the underlined portion?
A) elegant and practical in that its fur can range in
B) elegant and practical, with fur that can range in
C) elegant and practical by having fur that can range in
D) elegantly and practically ranged with fur in

27

A) NO CHANGE
B) have
C) had
D) will have

CONTINUE

While it is true that the Lynx is a carnivore, [28] it does not, as a rule, attack domestic beasts. Nor does it attack humans, though humans, sadly, have often hunted it.

At present, the lynx is third, after the brown bear and the gray wolf, on the list of endangered species for North America and Europe. [29] Its can still be found in the more remote areas of Norway and Sweden and in several of the Baltic countries, but it is already almost extinct elsewhere. In Britain, the lynx population was wiped out in the seventeenth century. In 1995, a report on the state of wildlife in Washington revealed that there were fewer than 250 lynx roaming the state. By 2000, in 49 of the 50 United States, the lynx was recorded as being threatened with extinction [30] and about to disappear. So much, perhaps, for its abilities of clairvoyance.

28
A) NO CHANGE
B) it does not as a rule,
C) it does not, as a rule
D) it does not; as a rule,

29
A) NO CHANGE
B) It's
C) They
D) It

30
A) NO CHANGE
B) and going to disappear.
C) and unable to live anymore.
D) DELETE the underlined portion.

Yet the existence of these conscientious lists of endangered species **31** reflect the new concern and attention that the lynx is garnering. There have been some attempts to re-establish the lynx in especially rugged parts of Europe. **32** In addition, in Colorado and the Rockies there has been a tentative reintroduction. Perhaps the lynx will flourish in such habitats, with only campers and mountain climbers for human company. **33**

31

A) NO CHANGE
B) reflects
C) are reflecting
D) reflected

32

The author is considering deleting the underlined sentence. Should the sentence be kept or deleted?

A) Kept, because the additional information supports the main idea of the paragraph.
B) Kept, because the lynx is more important in the United States than in Europe.
C) Deleted, because mentioning areas outside Europe distracts from the author's argument.
D) Deleted, because it reiterates information that appears in an earlier paragraph.

33

At this point, the writer is considering adding the following sentence.

> At present, the lynx is not common in zoos and wildlife parks, but could soon become a popular fixture at such attractions.

Should the writer make this addition here?

A) Yes, because it reinforces the author's other ideas about wildlife conservation.
B) Yes, because it indicates that contemporary ecologists are interested further study of the lynx.
C) No, because it undermines the passage's claim that the lynx will soon become extinct.
D) No, because distracts from the paragraph's discussion of efforts to reintroduce the lynx.

CONTINUE

Questions 34-44 are based on the following passage and supplementary material.

Economic Cycles

In the limited space of an urban environment, bicyclists and automobile drivers can at times feel at odds with one another. Cars can pose a serious threat to cyclists: one study performed in 2008 and 2009 found that **34** over 2,000 cyclists had been recently injured in Toronto and Vancouver. Risk can be a deterrent for many potential cyclists, even though bicycles are an environmentally friendly and physically invigorating form of urban transit.

34

Which choice provides the most accurate and relevant information from the graph?

A) NO CHANGE

B) the safest city for cyclists is Calgary.

C) more injuries and fatalities from cycling occur in Canada than in any other country.

D) at least 1,000 cyclists are killed each year in Toronto, Vancouver, Ottawa, and Winnipeg.

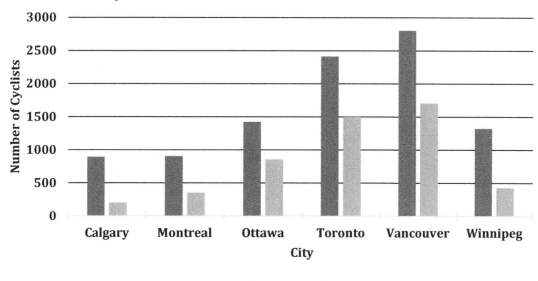

Cyclist Accidents in Selected Cities, 2008-2009

John [35] Forester, a cyclist and urban planner asserted decades ago that the safest and most effective way for cars and bicycles to share the road is for cyclists to behave like car drivers and take up part of the main roadway. In many cities in the U.S., this practice remains the norm. However, not all cyclists agree with Forester, and sometimes roadway sharing can lead to accidents: for example, [36] drivers who are used to seeing bikers on the road are more likely to pay attention and yield to those cyclists.

Today, many cyclists prefer commuting options such as bike lanes separated from main [37] roadways, and such lanes are built at the expense of valuable car parking spaces. Business owners [38] being worried that converting parking spaces into bike lanes is economically unwise, since limited parking would cause consumers to migrate to new businesses or to just stay home. [39] Yet this worry turns out to be unfounded. It turns out that cyclists spend roughly the same amount as drivers. In fact, as a 2012 survey of New York City residents revealed, cyclists

[35]
A) NO CHANGE
B) Forester, a cyclist and urban planner,
C) Forester—a cyclist and urban planner
D) Forester: a cyclist and urban planner,

[36]
Which choice provides the most relevant detail?
A) NO CHANGE
B) a cyclist in a dedicated bike lane may become complacent and crash due to lack of attention.
C) a cyclist who decides to coast through a stop sign to save energy runs the risk of colliding with an oncoming car.
D) it is a fairly common occurrence for speeding cars to crash into the median of a highway.

[37]
A) NO CHANGE
B) roadway's, and
C) roadway's, though
D) roadways, though

[38]
A) NO CHANGE
B) worried
C) were worrying
D) worry

[39]
Which choice most effectively combines the two underlined sentences?
A) Yet this worry turns out to be unfounded, it turns out that cyclists spend roughly the same amount as drivers.
B) Yet this worry is unfounded: cyclists spend roughly the same amount as drivers.
C) Yet this worry about cyclists is unfounded, spending roughly the same amount as drivers.
D) Yet this worry has turned out to be unfounded, so cyclists spend roughly the same amount as drivers.

CONTINUE

outspend drivers by $20 per capita. [40] Although, as one study in Melbourne, Australia, demonstrated, even if each cyclist [41] were to spend less money in one trip than each driver, merchants still would see net revenue increases, since approximately six bicycles can park in the space allotted to one car.

Research such as this indicates that both cyclists and automobile drivers can have a positive impact on neighborhood economics. The challenge for U.S. cities [42] are to provide safe passage for cyclists within existing infrastructure so that bicycles can travel without facing the perils of parking cars, intermittently stopping buses, and other automobile-related hazards. Bike lanes may be the answer: a 2010 study of the Vancouver area found that using separate bike lanes presented only 10% of the risk of cycling on main roadways.

In New York City, the years 2006-2010 saw major progress in bike infrastructure; [43] with the city now containing more than 400 miles of bike lanes today. By adding even more protected lanes, the city can both protect its cyclists [44] as well as work towards a major transportation target—bicycle usage that accounts for 6% of all trips within the city.

40
A) NO CHANGE
B) Furthermore,
C) Since
D) Whereas,

41
A) NO CHANGE
B) spend
C) had spent
D) having spent

42
A) NO CHANGE
B) are providing
C) is the provision of
D) is to provide

43
A) NO CHANGE
B) the city currently contains
C) the city contains
D) the city containing

44
A) NO CHANGE
B) and
C) plus
D) also

STOP
If you finish before time is called, you may check your work on this section only.
Do not turn to any other section.

Answer Key: TEST 2

Test 2

READING: SECTION 1

PASSAGE 1 Fiction	**PASSAGE 2** Social Science	**PASSAGE 3** Natural Science 1	**PASSAGE 4** Global Conversation	**PASSAGE 5** Natural Science 2
1. C	11. B	22. D	33. D	43. A
2. A	12. C	23. C	34. C	44. A
3. D	13. B	24. B	35. A	45. B
4. C	14. D	25. B	36. A	46. D
5. A	15. A	26. C	37. B	47. D
6. C	16. A	27. A	38. D	48. C
7. A	17. B	28. B	39. A	49. D
8. D	18. D	29. C	40. B	50. C
9. D	19. D	30. D	41. B	51. A
10. B	20. C	31. D	42. B	52. C
	21. D	32. A		

GRAMMAR: SECTION 2

PASSAGE 1 Keeping Your Cool with Hot-Desking	**PASSAGE 2** Pantomime Time	**PASSAGE 3** Finding the Missing Lynx	**PASSAGE 4** Economic Cycles
1. D	12. C	23. A	34. A
2. C	13. B	24. C	35. B
3. B	14. D	25. C	36. C
4. D	15. D	26. B	37. D
5. A	16. B	27. B	38. D
6. B	17. D	28. A	39. B
7. C	18. B	29. D	40. B
8. A	19. C	30. D	41. A
9. B	20. B	31. B	42. D
10. B	21. A	32. A	43. C
11. C	22. C	33. D	44. B

Once you have determined how many questions
you answered correctly, consult the chart on Page 156
to determine **your scaled SAT Verbal score.**

Please visit **ies2400.com/answers** for answer explanations.

Post-Test Analysis

This post-test analysis is essential if you want to see an improvement on your next test. Possible reasons for errors on the Reading and Grammar passages in this test are listed here. Place check marks next to the types of errors that pertain to you, or write your own types of errors in the blank spaces.

TIMING AND ACCURACY

◇ Spent too long reading individual passages
◇ Spent too long answering each question
◇ Spent too long on a few difficult questions
◇ Felt rushed and made silly mistakes or random errors
◇ Unable to work quickly using error types and POE
Other: _____

APPROACHING THE PASSAGES AND QUESTIONS

◇ Unable to effectively grasp a passage's tone or style
◇ Unable to effectively grasp a passage's topic or stance
◇ Did not understand the context of line references or underlined portions
◇ Did not eliminate false answers using strong evidence
◇ Answered questions using first impressions instead of POE
◇ Answered questions without checking or inserting final answer
◇ Eliminated correct answer during POE
Other: _____

> **Use this form** to better analyze your performance. If you don't understand why you made errors, there is no way that you can correct them!

READING TEST: # CORRECT_____ # WRONG _____ # OMITTED _____

◇ Interpreted passages rather than working with evidence
◇ Used outside knowledge rather than working with evidence
◇ Unable to effectively identify a passage's purpose or argument
◇ Unable to work effectively with word in context questions
◇ Unable to work effectively with questions about structure and writing technique
◇ Unable to work accurately or efficiently with Command of Evidence questions
◇ Unable to draw logical conclusions based on the content of the passages
◇ Difficulties understanding graphics and relating them to the passages
Other: _____

GRAMMAR TEST: # CORRECT_____ # WRONG _____ # OMITTED _____

◇ Did not identify proper verb number, form, or tense
◇ Did identify proper pronoun agreement or pronoun form (subject/object, who/which/where)
◇ Did not test for proper comparison phrasing (amount/number, between/among)
◇ Did not test phrase for correct adverb/adjective usage
◇ Did not see broader sentence structure (parallelism, misplaced modifier)
◇ Did not see flaws in punctuation (colon, semicolon, comma splice, misplaced commas)
◇ Did not see tricky possessives or contractions (its/it's, your/you're)
◇ Did not identify flaws in standard phrases (either . . . or, not only . . . but also, etc.)
◇ Did not use proper phrasing in sentences requiring the subjunctive
◇ Did not notice wordiness, redundancy, or faulty idioms
◇ Did not notice excessively informal expressions or flaws in essay style
◇ Created the wrong relationship between two sentences or two paragraphs
◇ Created the wrong placement for an out-of-order paragraph
◇ Did not properly read or analyze an insertion/deletion question
◇ Did not properly read or analyze the information in a graphic
◇ Understood a graphic, but could not identify the correct passage content
Other: _____

Test3

Reading Test
65 MINUTES, 52 QUESTIONS

Turn to Section 1 of your answer sheet to answer the questions in this section.

Each passage or pair of passages below is followed by a number of questions. After reading each passage or pair, choose the best answer to each question based on what is stated or implied in the passage or passages and in any accompanying graphics (such as a table or graph).

Questions 1-10 are based on the following passage.

Adapted from *A Room with a View* by E.M. Forster (1908). In this scene, a young Englishwoman named Lucy Honeychurch is visiting Florence with an older relative, Miss Bartlett.

It was pleasant to wake up in Florence, to open the eyes upon a bright bare room, with a floor of red tiles which look clean though they are not, with a painted ceiling whereon pink
Line griffins and blue amorini sport in a forest of yellow violins
5 and bassoons. It was pleasant, too, to fling wide the windows, pinching the fingers in unfamiliar fastenings, to lean out into sunshine with beautiful hills and trees and marble churches opposite, and close below, the Arno, gurgling against the embankment of the road.
10   Over the river men were at work with spades and sieves on the sandy foreshore, and on the river was a boat, also diligently employed for some mysterious end. An electric tram came rushing underneath the window. No one was inside it, except one tourist, but its platforms were overflowing with Italians,
15 who preferred to stand. Children tried to hang on behind, and the conductor, with no malice, spat in their faces to make them let go. Then soldiers appeared—good-looking, undersized men—wearing each a knapsack covered with mangy fur, and a great-coat which had been cut for some larger soldier. Beside
20 them walked officers, looking foolish and fierce, and before them went little boys, turning somersaults in time with the band. The tramcar became entangled in their ranks, and moved on painfully, like a caterpillar in a swarm of ants. One of the little boys fell down, and some white bullocks came out of an
25 archway. Indeed, if it had not been for the good advice of an old man who was selling button-hooks, the road might never have got clear.

Over such trivialities as these many a valuable hour may slip away, and the traveler who has gone to Italy to study the
30 tactile values of Giotto, or the corruption of the Papacy, may return remembering nothing but the blue sky and the men and women who live under it. So it was as well that Miss Bartlett should tap and come in, and having commented on Lucy's leaving the door unlocked, and on her leaning out of the
35 window before she was fully dressed, should urge her to hasten herself, or the best of the day would be gone. By the time Lucy was ready her cousin had done her breakfast, and was listening to a third one of the hotel's guests, a clever lady, among the crumbs.
40   A conversation then ensued, on not unfamiliar lines. Miss Bartlett was, after all, a wee bit tired, and thought they had better spend the morning settling; unless Lucy would at all like to go out? Lucy would rather like to go out, as it was her first day in Florence, but, of course, she could go alone. Miss
45 Bartlett could not allow this. Of course she would accompany Lucy everywhere. Oh, certainly not; Lucy would stop with her cousin. Oh, no! that would never do. Oh, yes!
     At this point the clever lady broke in.
     "If it is Mrs. Grundy who is troubling you, I do assure
50 you that you can neglect the good person. Being English, Miss Honeychurch will be perfectly safe. Italians understand. A dear friend of mine, Contessa Baroncelli, has two daughters, and when she cannot send a maid to school with them, she lets them go in sailor-hats instead. Every one takes them for
55 English, you see, especially if their hair is strained tightly behind."
     Miss Bartlett was unconvinced by the safety of Contessa Baroncelli's daughters. She was determined to take Lucy herself, her head not being so very bad. The clever lady then
60 said that she was going to spend a long morning in Santa Croce, and if Lucy would come too, she would be delighted.

CONTINUE

"I will take you by a dear dirty back way, Miss Honeychurch, and if you bring me luck, we shall have an adventure."

65   Lucy said that this was most kind, and at once opened the Baedeker, to see where Santa Croce was.

"Tut, tut! Miss Lucy!" Thus said her clever companion "I hope we shall soon emancipate you from Baedeker. He does but touch the surface of things. As to the true Italy—he does
70 not even dream of it. The true Italy is only to be found by patient observation."

1

It can be reasonably inferred from the passage that Lucy is

A) an expatriate who wishes to make Florence her home.

B) a tourist visiting Florence with her husband.

C) an academic studying politics in Italy.

D) a person who has limited familiarity with Florence.

2

Which choice provides the best evidence for the answer to the previous question?

A) Lines 28-32 ("Over such . . . under it")

B) Lines 43-44 ("Lucy would . . . go alone")

C) Lines 51-54 ("A dear friend . . . . instead")

D) Lines 68-71 ("He does . . . observation")

3

The author repeats the phrase "It was pleasant" in lines 1 and 5 primarily in order to

A) emphasize the hedonism of the central character.

B) contrast the charms of one city with the unpleasantness of another.

C) introduce a detailed description of a setting.

D) foreshadow a later criticism of Florentine society.

4

The metaphor "a caterpillar in a swarm of ants" (line 23) indicates that the observer is

A) critical of the slow pace of Florentine traffic.

B) appalled at the recklessness of those who are walking on the tracks.

C) detached from the scene as though watching another species.

D) wary of utilizing public transportation in Florence for fear of injury.

5

The observation in lines 28-32 ("Over such . . . under it") primarily serves to

A) indicate that the novelty and distraction found in Italy are unique.

B) transition from an impressionistic account to a social encounter.

C) enumerate the reasons why a person may travel to Italy.

D) allude to the effects of Giotto's artistic methods on foreign paintings.

6

Miss Bartlett's behavior in lines 45-47 ("Of course . . . yes!") is best characterized as

A) abrasive disregard.

B) delicate suggestion.

C) shy curiosity.

D) aggressive solicitude.

7

The clever lady mentions Contessa Baroncelli's children to make the point that

A) children are rarely bothered in Italian cities.

B) Italians are easily confused with the English.

C) it is inappropriate for a maid to accompany English children.

D) Lucy Honeychurch does not need an escort in Florence because she is English.

8

Why does the "clever companion" (line 67) wish to "emancipate" (line 68) Lucy from her guidebook?

A) To convince Lucy to ignore Miss Bartlett

B) Because Baedecker does an especially poor job of cataloging Italian art and culture

C) Because Baedecker does not relate an authentic version of Florence

D) To free Lucy of the negative opinion of Italians fostered by Baedecker's guidebook

9

The author would likely agree that "patient observation" (line 71) is best represented by

A) an exhaustive tour of museums, chapels, and other sites of historical interest.

B) a detailed study of the artistic nuances epitomized by the works of Giotto.

C) a profound understanding of the Italians' deep nobility of spirit.

D) a leisurely exploration of the daily scenes of Florentine life.

10

Which choice provides the best evidence for the answer to the previous question?

A) Lines 5-9 ("It was pleasant . . . of the road")

B) Lines 13-15 ("No one . . . preferred to stand")

C) Lines 40-43 ("A conversation . . . go out?")

D) Lines 57-59 ("Miss Bartlett . . . so very bad")

Questions 11-20 are based on the following passages.

The passages below, adapted from works published in 2012, discuss in-school bullying and how this problem has recently been addressed.

Passage 1

It's no secret that getting bullied is hurtful. But when a student, or any individual, gets bullied in person, there's only so much damage a bully can do before the possibility of someone
Line stepping in arises. Yet in cyberspace, bullying takes on a whole
5 new meaning. Now, perpetrators can gain momentum as others chime in as well. And those others who do decide to join the bullying don't need to leave the ease and comfort of their chairs; they simply press a few buttons on their keyboards and they're done. But the impact for those who are bullied is lasting.
10 Bullying is just as much a public health problem as it is a victim's or individual's problem, as it causes major concerns for entire school environments. High schools with a high rate of bullying have scored much lower on standardized tests than those with lower rates of bullying. These lower
15 test scores affect a given school's capacity to meet federal requirements and hinder the education of the many students who do not pass the exams. This is a problem for schools on account of the No Child Left Behind Act, under which students must receive passing scores on standardized tests to
20 even graduate. Under this act, schools are now under pressure to do something urgent about bullying.
To stop bullying, we need to work together to educate everyone and get everyone involved: administrators, parents, and students. President Barack Obama recently started a campaign
25 against bullying and Lady Gaga has her own foundation, called Born This Way, to help spread the message. But these are just a few outlets, and unless society as a whole does what is needed to combat this problem, the consequences of bullying will only grow worse. We do not permit harassment and the abuse of
30 adults in the workplace, so why should similar protections not be afforded to children in school?

Passage 2

After school specials are not as popular now as they were in the 1980's, but those who watched them can recall at least one or two specials on bullying. But what some seem to forget is that
35 bullying has been around long before the media put it in the hot seat. Bullying has not gotten worse over the years, according to studies in the field; rather, the media attention it has received, as a product of the devastating results of bullying, has highlighted this major problem.
40 According to StopBullying.gov, a popular website that tracks bullying, "Bullying is unwanted, aggressive behavior . . . that involves a real or perceived power imbalance. The behavior is repeated, or has the potential to be repeated,

CONTINUE

over time. Bullying includes actions such as making threats,
45 spreading rumors, attacking someone physically or verbally,
and excluding someone from a group on purpose." The
argument that these instances are simply cases of "children
being children" is no longer a viable excuse. In an age of
interconnectedness, bullying delivers easy and immediate
50 pain. The perpetrators don't have to pose a physical threat at
all; they now have the Internet at their disposal and can do
their damage without leaving the comfort of their own homes.
    The act of bullying doesn't only have an effect on the victim.
For the perpetrators, bullying can be the beginning of a trajectory
55 of trouble, including disorderly conduct, skipping school,
substance abuse, and, quite possibly, adult criminal behavior.
For the victims, being bullied leads not simply to immediate
physical and emotional pain; many times, the impact can extend
into later life. The scars don't go away, but stay with the victims
60 into adulthood. The ripple effect doesn't stop at the bully and the
bullied, either, since those who are simply witnesses and are not
directly involved in bullying are more likely to skip school or
abuse alcohol. A climate of fear affects everyone.
    Unfortunately, the old way of doing things (suspension and
65 expulsion) doesn't stop bullying. Punishment-based strategies
don't give students the tools they need to make lasting behavioral
changes. Those who have a tendency to victimize others usually
have weak social skills and little emotional regulation, which
can definitely be contributors to bullying behaviors. Therefore,
70 the best strategy for combating bullying is a comprehensive
approach. This includes getting the bullies involved. It may
sound counterintuitive, but the bullies need help too, maybe the
most help. If we can get through to them, we can come close to
eliminating the problem altogether.

11

As used in line 31, "afforded" most nearly means

A) managed.
B) provided.
C) donated.
D) paid.

12

As used in line 48, "viable" most nearly means

A) developed.
B) successful.
C) vital.
D) adequate.

13

In Passage 1, the author implies that schools are working
to address bullying partially because

A) schools are increasingly aware of the negative and
long-lasting consequences of bullying.
B) federal legislation obligates schools to be more
concerned about bullying.
C) parents are becoming more vocal about making schools
into bully-free environments.
D) bullying in school is significantly more severe than
bullying in cyberspace.

14

Which choice provides the best evidence for the answer to
the previous question?

A) Lines 4-5 ("Yet in cyberspace . . . meaning")
B) Lines 10-11 ("Bullying is . . . problem")
C) Lines 20-21 ("Under . . . bullying")
D) Lines 22-23 ("To stop . . . involved")

15

How would the author of Passage 2 most likely respond to
point made in the final paragraph of Passage 1?

A) Victims should be protected from bullying, but the
perpetrators must be given constructive attention.
B) The problem of Internet-based bullying needs to be
addressed as a public health concern.
C) It is unnecessary to focus primarily on protecting
children from bullies at school.
D) Drawing parallels between the workplace and the
school removes focus from issues unique to children.

16

Which choice provides the best evidence for the answer to
the previous question?

A) Lines 34-36 ("But what . . . hot seat")
B) Lines 50-52 ("The perpetrators . . . homes")
C) Lines 65-67 ("Punishment-based . . . changes")
D) Lines 71-73 ("It may . . . most help")

CONTINUE 77

17

Which best describes the overall relationship between Passage 1 and Passage 2?

A) Passage 2 addresses a different aspect of the issue presented in Passage 1.

B) Passage 2 calls into question the central points advanced in Passage 1.

C) Passage 2 argues against the effectiveness of the solution proposed in Passage 1.

D) Passage 2 analyzes a dilemma described in more general terms in Passage 1.

18

The central claim of Passage 2 is that bullying

A) can be defined in multiple ways depending on the circumstances.

B) negatively affects perpetrators, victims, and bystanders.

C) must be directly addressed by the government.

D) is unrelated to the declining popularity of after school specials.

19

On which of the following points would the authors of both passages most likely agree?

A) Punishment is an effective way to make schools safer.

B) Bullying behavior suggests underlying psychological issues.

C) Receiving lower test scores correlates with being bullied.

D) The Internet plays a role in facilitating bullying.

20

What function does the quotation in lines 41-46 serve in Passage 2?

A) It examines the consequences of a problem discussed in the previous paragraph.

B) It offers evidence for a claim made in the previous paragraph.

C) It clarifies a term that appears in the previous paragraph.

D) It rejects a major assumption of the previous paragraph.

Questions 21-31 are based on the following passage and supplementary material.

The following passage is taken from an article on new medicines that are being used to combat diseases that affect the human eye.

Imagine that you are wearing sunglasses. Everything you see is darkened because you are looking not only through your eyes' own lenses as usual, but also through the dark lenses
Line of the sunglasses. Now imagine that you are looking through
5 sunglasses coated in white paint. You would not able to see anything clearly, perhaps only vague shadows and light spots. Millions of people live with this reality in the form of cataracts, white cloudy formations in the eye.

Cataracts are formed when crystallins (which, in their
10 normal state, help the eye to maintain its transparency and structure) clump together and obscure the lens of the eye. Although their formation is not fully understood, cataracts are very common and tend to affect older people. According to the National Eye Institute, most Americans who are at least
15 80 years old have, or have had, cataracts. The only current treatment for cataracts is eye surgery; unfortunately, many people, particularly those living in economically disadvantaged countries, do not have access to this procedure. Without surgery, cataracts can thicken and cause blindness. In fact,
20 according to the Fred Hollows Foundation, cataracts are responsible for approximately half of all cases of blindness in the world.

Despite the increasing correlation of cataract frequency and old age, some forms of cataracts are genetic and appear in
25 children. Ling Zhao, a molecular biologist from the University of California, decided to study children with inherited forms of cataracts in the hopes of discovering what causes cataract formation. Her research team discovered that these children have a genetic mutation that prevents their bodies from
30 producing lanosterol, a steroid normally found in humans.

One of the researchers who has worked alongside Zhao is Dr. Kang Zhang, a professor of ophthalmology at the University of California. Zhang explained that, "by screening families across the world for mutations that affect vision, we
35 found four kids in two families with genetic aberrations in an enzyme called lanosterol synthase." As its name suggests, lanosterol synthase synthesizes lanosterol. Dr. Zhao's team then hypothesized that perhaps a lack of lanosterol, caused by the absence of lanosterol synthase, was responsible for cataract
40 formation.

To evaluate this hypothesis, the researchers tested lanosterol eye drops on lab models of human lens cells clouded by cataracts. The results, which showed clear diminution of cataract thickness, were dramatic. The scientists then tested the
45 eye drops on rabbits with severe cataracts. After six days, 11 out of the 13 rabbits had very mild cataracts or exhibited

CONTINUE

completely clear eyes. The team then tested the eye drops on dogs, with very similar results.

50 Dr. Zhao and her team published their results in the scientific journal *Nature* in July 2015. The findings led molecular biologist and cataract researcher Jonathan King of the Massachusetts Institute of Technology (MIT) to exclaim, "This is a really comprehensive and compelling paper—the strongest I've seen of its kind in a decade."

55 In addition to its potential to treat animals, lanosterol holds a lot of promise as a human medicine. If the drops work as well for human patients as they did for the rabbits and dogs, the eye drops would not only save millions of people from the cost and inconvenience of surgery, but also save the eyesight
60 of millions more who do not have access to cataract surgery. Clara Eaglen of the Royal National Institute of Blind People remarked, "Anything that removes the need for invasive surgery will be hugely beneficial to patients. If eye drops could be self-administered, this would remove the burden on
65 eye clinics." It is possible, now, to imagine a world without cataracts.

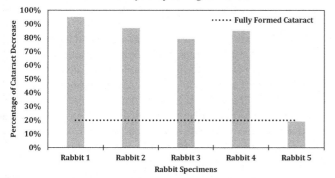

Lanosterol Eye Drop Testing on Rabbits

21

The primary purpose of the first paragraph is to

A) advocate for those living with blindness.

B) illustrate the process of cataract formation.

C) demonstrate the effect of cataracts on vision.

D) introduce a research project conducted at MIT.

22

According to the research discussed in the passage, it can most reasonably be inferred that cataracts form due to

A) complications in surgery.

B) over-activity of enzymes.

C) lower hygienic standards.

D) a steroid deficiency.

23

The primary purpose of the quotation in lines 53-54 is to

A) add legitimacy to Dr. Zhao's findings.

B) undermine a dissenting opinion.

C) give further insight into the cause of cataracts.

D) suggest that Jonathan King and Ling Zhao will eventually collaborate.

24

Childhood cataracts are different from adult cataracts because they

A) are explained largely by heredity.

B) do not lead to blindness.

C) are more common in males.

D) have been ignored by researchers

25

Which choice provides the best evidence for the answer to the previous question?

A) Lines 15-16 ("The only . . . surgery")

B) Lines 19-22 ("In fact . . . the world")

C) Lines 23-25 ("Despite . . . children")

D) Lines 41-43 ("To evaluate . . . cataracts")

26

According to the passage, the treatment of cataracts with lanosterol

A) has not yet been proven effective for humans.

B) cannot replace traditional methods.

C) could cause more complications than surgery.

D) causes thickening of the lens of the eye.

CONTINUE

27

Which choice provides the best evidence for the answer to the previous question?

A) Lines 44-45 ("The scientists . . . cataracts")

B) Lines 49-50 ("Dr. Zhao . . . July 2015")

C) Lines 56-60 ("If the drops . . . surgery")

D) Lines 65-66 ("It is . . . cataracts")

28

As used in line 35, "aberrations" most nearly means

A) misinterpretations.

B) anomalies.

C) refractions.

D) idiosyncrasies.

29

As used in line 43, "diminution" most nearly means

A) removal.

B) reduction.

C) depletion.

D) depreciation.

30

Based on the graph, which rabbit from the experiment would provide the weakest evidence for the author's claims?

A) Rabbit 1

B) Rabbit 2

C) Rabbit 4

D) Rabbit 5

31

How does the graph corroborate the findings of Dr. Zhao and her team?

A) It indicates that lanosterol treatment is most effective for large mammals.

B) It indicates that lanosterol treatment can be frequently though not absolutely effective.

C) It indicates that lanosterol treatment has no adverse side-effects for mammal species.

D) It indicates that lanosterol treatment will always improve a patient's vision.

Questions 32-42 are based on the following passage

The following is an excerpt from the book *Anarchism and Other Essays* by Emma Goldman (1869-1940), a proponent of political anarchism who relocated from Europe to the U.S. (The term "anarchism" refers to a school of thought that radically opposes government intervention in day-to-day life—and that, at its most extreme, supports the abolition of formal government.)

It is generally conceded that unless the returns of any business venture exceed the cost, bankruptcy is inevitable. But those engaged in the business of producing wealth have
Line not yet learned even this simple lesson. Every year the cost
5   of production in human life is growing larger (50,000 killed, 100,000 wounded in America last year); the returns to the masses, who help to create wealth, are ever getting smaller. Ye America continues to be blind to the inevitable bankruptcy of our business of production. Nor is this the only crime of the
10 latter. Still more fatal is the crime of turning the producer into a mere particle of a machine, with less will and decision than his master of steel and iron. Man is being robbed not merely of the products of his labor, but of the power of free initiative, of originality, and the interest in, or desire for, the things he is
15 making.

Real wealth consists in things of utility and beauty, in things that help to create strong, beautiful bodies and surroundings inspiring to live in. But if man is doomed to wind cotton around a spool, or dig coal, or build roads for
20 thirty years of his life, there can be no talk of wealth. What he gives to the world is only gray and hideous things, reflecting a dull and hideous existence—too weak to live, too cowardly to die. Strange to say, there are people who extol this deadening method of centralized production as the proudest achievement
25 of our age. They fail utterly to realize that if we are to continue in machine subserviency, our slavery is more complete than was our bondage to the King. They do not want to know that centralization is not only the death-knell of liberty, but also of health and beauty, of art and science, all these being impossibl
30 in a clock-like, mechanical atmosphere.

Anarchism cannot but repudiate such a method of production: its goal is the freest possible expression of all the latent powers of the individual. Oscar Wilde defines a perfect personality as "one who develops under perfect conditions,
35 who is not wounded, maimed, or in danger." A perfect personality, then, is only possible in a state of society where man is free to choose the mode of work, the conditions of work, and the freedom to work. One to whom the making of a table, the building of a house, or the tilling of the soil, is what
40 the painting is to the artist and the discovery to the scientist— the result of inspiration, of intense longing, and deep interest i work as a creative force. That being the ideal of Anarchism, it

CONTINUE

economic arrangements must consist of voluntary productive and distributive associations, gradually developing into free
45 communism, as the best means of producing with the least waste of human energy. Anarchism, however, also recognizes the right of the individual, or numbers of individuals, to arrange at all times for other forms of work, in harmony with their tastes and desires.
50 Such free display of human energy being possible only under complete individual and social freedom, Anarchism directs its forces against the third and greatest foe of all social equality: namely, the State, organized authority, or statutory law—the dominion of human conduct.
55 Just as religion has fettered the human mind, and as property, or the monopoly of things, has subdued and stifled man's needs, so has the State enslaved his spirit, dictating every phase of conduct. "All government in essence," says Emerson, "is tyranny." It matters not whether it is government
60 by divine right or majority rule. In every instance its aim is the absolute subordination of the individual.
Referring to the American government, the greatest American Anarchist, David Thoreau, said: "Government, what is it but a tradition, though a recent one, endeavoring to
65 transmit itself unimpaired to posterity, but each instance losing its integrity; it has not the vitality and force of a single living man. Law never made man a whit more just; and by means of their respect for it, even the well disposed are daily made agents of injustice."

32

As used in line 11, "will" most nearly means

A) character.

B) insistence.

C) volition.

D) desire.

33

The author most strongly implies which of the following about "the power of free initiative" (line 13)?

A) It is not valued in the current business of production.

B) It is thriving because of the mechanization of labor.

C) It never contributed significantly to productivity.

D) It is a serious threat to the centralized economy.

34

Goldman describes those who do not share her viewpoint as

A) selfish.

B) irresponsible.

C) oblivious.

D) uncreative.

35

Which choice provides the best evidence for the answer to the previous question?

A) Lines 1-2 ("It is generally . . . is inevitable")

B) Lines 20-23 ("What he gives . . . cowardly to die")

C) Lines 25-27 ("They fail utterly . . . to the King")

D) Lines 67-69 ("Law never made . . . injustice")

36

Goldman presents "the proudest achievement of our age" (lines 24-25) as a characterization that

A) is used by those who do not agree with her.

B slightly overstates the country's progress.

C) is used by those who have acquired great wealth.

D) accurately depicts the current economic system.

37

As used in line 26, "complete" most nearly means

A) unmodified.

B) total.

C) exhaustive.

D) finished.

38

The discussion of work in lines 38-42 ("One to whom . . . creative force") primarily serves to

A) demonstrate that it is unlikely that most people enjoy their jobs.

B) describe the manner in which work should be approached.

C) call attention to particular vocations that have recently been neglected.

D) emphasize that working with machines would streamline certain processes.

39

According to the Goldman, what is an advantage of Anarchism?

A) It fosters the consolidation of wealth among few individuals.

B) It frees citizens from a violently oppressive central government.

C) It gives people freedom to make personal decisions about work.

D) It establishes regulations to organize production and trade organizations.

40

Which choice provides the best evidence for the answer to the previous question?

A) Lines 16-18 ("Real wealth . . . to live in")

B) Lines 46-49 ("Anarchism . . . and desires")

C) Lines 50-54 ("Such free . . . human conduct")

D) Lines 62-67 ("Referring to . . . living man")

41

As they are presented in the passage, Emerson and Thoreau would most probably view the United States federal government as

A) detrimental.

B) legitimate.

C) prejudiced.

D) revolutionary.

42

Goldman contends in the passage that individuals are profoundly influenced by

A) the environment where they are normally employed.

B) the growing recognition that government is unjust.

C) the ideas of respected thinkers and philosophers.

D) the desire to make government smaller but more efficient.

Questions 43-52 are based on the following passage and supplementary material.

The following passage is from an article about the effects of industrial agriculture on the atmosphere.

Greenhouse gases like carbon dioxide (CO_2), methane (CH_4), and nitrous oxide (N_2O) absorb infrared light and warm the globe. They are also all components of biological cycles:
Line CO_2 is consumed in photosynthesis and emitted in animal
5 respiration; N_2O is one component of the nitrogen cycle; CH_4 is consumed and emitted by certain species of microorganisms. In balance with their natural cycles and at relatively constant atmospheric concentrations, these gases have kept the earth habitable. But industrialization has increased the concentration
10 of each substance.

Current agricultural practices exacerbate the problem. For example, soil naturally holds carbon, which in turn helps the soil retain nutrients, filter water, and regulate temperature. In fact, soil holds three times more carbon than does the atmosphere.
15 But today's commercial farmers use chemical fertilizers and pesticides that deplete the soil's carbon-capturing ability. About one third of the excess carbon in the atmosphere can be attributed to mismanaged and destroyed soils.

Our current food system also affects CH_4 concentration.
20 Methanogens (CH_4-producing microorganisms) live in the guts of cows, termites, and even humans, helping us break down and absorb our food. Digestion creates CH_4 for release into the atmosphere, and U.S. cattle contribute 20 percent of emissions. This could be reduced: most commercially raised cattle subsist
25 on grain, which forces the digestive system to work harder, leading to more CH_4. To see how diet affects CH_4, Stonyfield Farm conducted a study wherein 15 Vermont farms added more grasses to their cows' grainy diets. This study and a similar one in France found a significant drop in methane emissions: as
30 much as 30 percent.

Industrial agriculture has an even greater effect on N_2O concentration. Commercial agriculture demands large amounts of ammonium-rich fertilizer. The natural nitrogen cycle produces ammonium, but not enough to support our large population. To
35 accommodate mega-farms, scientists discovered how to create fixed nitrogen on a commercial scale. This industrial "Haber-Bosch" process is energy intensive and bad for the environment. In fact, synthetic nitrogen fertilizers account for 69 percent of N_2O emissions in the U.S.
40   When the elements of today's food system are added up— deforestation, land use change, food processing, transportation, refrigeration, packaging, retail, food waste, and agriculture itself—they comprise between 44 and 57 percent of global human-sourced greenhouse gas emissions. Some might shrug
45 this off, suggesting that today's methods are more efficient than those of the past. Actually, the reverse is true. In 1940, 1 calorie

CONTINUE ➡

of energy produced 2.3 calories of food. Today, 10 calories of energy produce less than half of that—just 1 calorie of food. Some will accept this inefficiency, touting the use of large farms, chemical products and uniform seeds to "feed the world." However, the relationship between food production and world hunger is unclear. We produce more food per capita today than at any time in history—about 4.3 pounds per person per day. Yet hunger persists.

The benefits of our current food system are unclear, but the environmental damage is starkly apparent. In the face of changing climate and potentially harsher farming conditions, it would be wise to start taking organic and local farms—those that prohibit chemicals, foster biodiversity, and heal the soil—more seriously.

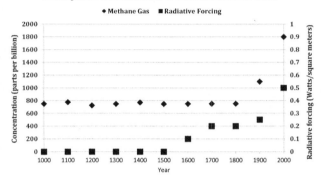

Atmospheric Concentration of Methane Gas Over Time

43

The primary purpose of the passage is to

A) summarize the effects of greenhouse gases on the environment.

B) introduce a new strategy for industrial-scale food production.

C) indicate that current agricultural practices have destructive side effects.

D) explain how human activity damages the natural carbon cycle.

44

Which choice provides the best evidence for the answer to the previous question?

A) Lines 15-16 ("But today's . . . ability")

B) Lines 34-36 ("To accommodate . . . scale")

C) Lines 40-44 ("When the . . . emissions")

D) Lines 49-50 ("Some will . . . the world")

45

As used in line 12, "holds" most nearly means

A) regards.

B) absorbs.

C) restrains.

D) dominates.

46

Based on the passage, which choice best describes the relationship between the research in Vermont and that in France?

A) The research in Vermont contradicts that in France.

B) The research in Vermont expands on that in France.

C) The research in France corrects that in Vermont.

D) The research in France corroborates that in Vermont.

47

As used in line 34, "support" most nearly means

A) condone.

B) finance.

C) comfort.

D) sustain.

48

In lines 44-46 ("Some might . . . the past"), what is the most likely reason the author mentions a potential opinion?

A) To anticipate a flawed counterargument

B) To concede an important point in a debate

C) To mock proponents of industrial efficiency

D) To validate a seeming misconception

49

Which choice provides the best evidence for the answer to the previous question?

A) Lines 9-10 ("But industrialization . . . each substance")

B) Line 46 ("Actually, the . . . true")

C) Lines 52-53 ("We produce . . . per day")

D) Lines 55-56 ("The benefits . . . apparent")

50

The passage and the accompanying graph most strongly suggest that the use of chemicals in agriculture has what effect?

A) Elimination of world hunger

B) Streamlined food production

C) Damage to the environment

D) Contaminated crop yields

51

Based on the graph, the ratio of methane gas concentration to radiative forcing was highest in what year?

A) 1600

B) 1700

C) 1900

D) 2000

52

It can reasonably be inferred from the passage and from the graph that

A) since 1800, the atmospheric concentration of methane has increased with a corresponding increase in radiative forcing.

B) since 1800, the atmospheric concentration of methane has increased while radiative forcing has remained constant.

C) since 1800, the atmospheric concentration of methane has decreased while radiative forcing has increased.

D) the atmospheric concentration and radiative forcing of methane have largely remained constant since 1000.

STOP

If you finish before time is called, you may check your work on this section only.

Do not turn to any other section.

No Test Material On This Page

Writing Test
35 MINUTES, 44 QUESTIONS

Turn to Section 2 of your answer sheet to answer the questions in this section.

Questions 1-11 are based on the following passage.

Mutual Attraction: New Magnetic Metals

— 1 —

Many aspects of modern technology rely on the use of magnets. Magnetic Resonance Imaging (MRI) technology uses magnets to obtain anatomical images, which facilitate diagnosis and treatment. Magnets inside credit cards allow these thin pieces of plastic to communicate valuable financial information. Computer memory storage requires magnets, and wind turbines transform wind into electricity using magnets. Yet only three of all known metals are permanently magnetic at room temperature: iron, nickel, and cobalt. Others can hold only a weak charge for a short period of time, so manufacturers rely **2** almost only exclusively on these three elements.

1
A) NO CHANGE
B) relies
C) to rely
D) relying

2
A) NO CHANGE
B) almost exclusively in only
C) only exclusively in
D) almost exclusively on

CONTINUE

— 2 —

While it is possible to turn a non-magnetic object containing iron, nickel, or cobalt into a magnet by passing a magnet over the object, the new technology requires a more specialized approach. The researchers coated thin pieces of copper and manganese with a special one-nanometer layer of organic molecules called "buckyballs." **3** Buckyballs are spheres made of 60 carbon atoms. The interaction between the metal and buckyball layers **4** transfer some electrons from the metal to the organic layer, and this change makes the metal magnetic.

— 3 —

The research team was indeed able to produce magnets, though these were relatively weak. Copper produced a stronger effect than manganese, yet was ten times weaker than nickel and thirty times weaker than iron. However, the significance of this research lies in the permanence of the magnetism, rather than **5** their strength, since **6** it shows that it is possible for scientists to **7** work around a supposedly intrinsic property of metals. One of the study's lead authors, Tim Moorsom, likens this breakthrough to mixing iron and carbon to produce steel, which is lighter and more flexible than iron, and therefore can be used in a different range of applications. This magnetizing technique, if it can be successfully applied to metals beyond copper and manganese, may prove to be just as useful when it comes to computing innovations.

3
The writer is considering deleting the underlined sentence. Should the sentence be kept or deleted?
A) Kept, because it supports the writer's claim that magnetizing metals is a simple process.
B) Kept, because it defines a term that is important in this paragraph.
C) Deleted, because it blurs the paragraph's focus by discussing a loosely related detail.
D) Deleted, because it provides information that is found earlier in the passage.

4
A) NO CHANGE
B) transferring
C) transfers
D) that transfer

5
A) NO CHANGE
B) its
C) its'
D) it's

6
A) NO CHANGE
B) this study
C) they
D) the team

7
A) NO CHANGE
B) make accommodations for
C) fight against
D) evade

— 4 —

Fatma Al Ma'Mari, another of the study's lead authors, **8** predict that computing will soon require new types of materials, including new magnets, to provide greater storage and processing abilities. **9** However, these small, efficient components may even make computers more environmentally friendly. Improved computing and storage ability combined with improved energy and material efficiency would be a positive step for technologies that are increasingly necessary for many industries.

— 5 —

A recent **10** breakthrough in materials, science may help to change this situation. In a 2015 study led by scientists at the University of Leeds, a research team was able to generate weak magnetism in two non-magnetic metals, copper and manganese. These elements are relatively abundant and the team's innovative technology could expand the range of possible metals used for magnetic applications.

Question 11 asks about the previous passage as a whole.

8

A) NO CHANGE
B) predicts
C) have predicted
D) predicting

9

A) NO CHANGE
B) Thereafter,
C) Furthermore,
D) So,

10

A) NO CHANGE
B) breakthrough in materials science, may help
C) breakthrough, in materials, science may help
D) breakthrough in materials science may help

Think about the previous passage as a whole as you answer question 11.

11

To make the passage most logical, paragraph 5 should be placed
A) where it is now.
B) after paragraph 1.
C) after paragraph 2.
D) after paragraph 3.

CONTINUE

Questions 12-22 are based on the following passage and supplementary material.

More Than One Way to Bounce a Dead Cat

    In 2014, electronics retailer RadioShack was well on <u>there</u> way to corporate catastrophe. The company's stock price had declined <u>from almost $3 per share in 2013 to a paltry $0.50 per share just two years later.</u> Yet there was a break from all this bad news when RadioShack stock experienced a brief period of recovery and, temporarily, reached a price of $1.00-1.50 per share in the summer of 2014. From there, the stock abruptly reversed course and <u>plummeted; the</u> company itself filed for bankruptcy in February of 2015.

12

A) NO CHANGE
B) its
C) it's
D) their

13

Which choice most accurately and effectively represents the information in the graph?

A) NO CHANGE
B) from its highest point to a paltry $0.50 per share just a year later.
C) from almost $5 per share in 2012 to a paltry $1.50 just two years later.
D) from almost $5 per share in 2012 to a paltry $0.50 per share just two years later.

14

A) NO CHANGE
B) plummeted, the
C) plummeted, but the
D) plummeted, with the

Radio Shack Stock Price

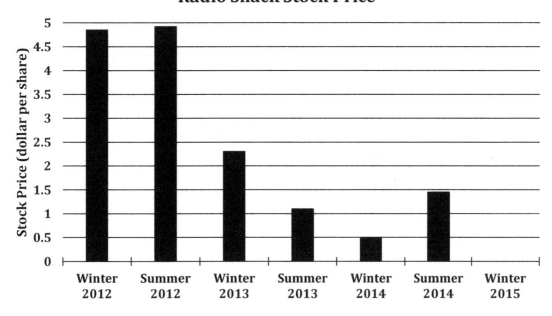

What happened to RadioShack in this brief reversal of ill fortune **15** <u>were</u> what economists call a "dead cat bounce." This phenomenon takes its name from the idea that even something as lifeless and useless **16** <u>than</u> a dead cat will bounce if dropped from a high enough elevation. **17** <u>The reasons for such a bounce are various.</u> In business, a spate of good press, a sudden investment, or the normal ups and downs of the stock market may "bounce" a company slightly higher; however, such a bounce should not obscure the overall and irreversible downtrend that, by definition, must accompany a "dead cat bounce."

Yet it is not uncommon for commentators **18** <u>interpreting</u> a "dead cat bounce" as a genuine business turnaround. One source of such mistaken interpretation is simply wishful thinking: after all, the glory days of a dying business can have a nostalgic value that clouds better judgment. Many Americans, **19** <u>for instance,</u> fondly remember how RadioShack flourished decades ago by selling electronic equipment to homeowners, hobbyists, and computer startups. Nobody would really want such a business to fail, even if it ultimately does. There is also the idea, equally prevalent but equally false, that a dead cat bounce represents an opportunity to profit. In truth, if you buy stock in a company that is experiencing such a bounce, you are buying into a small, hard-to-gauge uptick and a larger pattern of decline.

15
A) NO CHANGE
B) being
C) is
D) are

16
A) NO CHANGE
B) for
C) to
D) as

17
The writer is considering deleting the underlined sentence. Should the writer do this?
A) Yes, because it merely reformulates the thought in the previous sentence.
B) Yes, because it undermines the writer's claims about the prevalence of dead cat bounces.
C) No, because it introduces the following sentence.
D) No, because it reinforces the writer's point that dead cat bounces are preventable.

18
A) NO CHANGE
B) to interpret
C) that interpret
D) when interpreting

19
A) NO CHANGE
B) however,
C) likewise,
D) regardless,

CONTINUE

[20] Dead cat bounces are notoriously difficult to spot. First, consider the market at large, and see if there is still healthy demand for the kind of goods and services a company provides: if such demand [21] will dry up, expect little more than a dead cat bounce. Second, look at the on-the-ground operations: a company that is single-mindedly downsizing its operations or changing leadership in a panic is probably headed nowhere but down. And third, [22] to keep in mind that turnaround success stories are much-publicized yet ultimately rare, while dead cat bounces—even though the press never reports most of them—abound.

20

Which choice most effectively sets up the paragraph?

A) NO CHANGE

B) So how can you decide whether a company is experiencing the beginning of a turnaround or simply a dead cat bounce?

C) So how can a company avoid experiencing a dead cat bounce, and acquire the investments necessary for a true business rebound?

D) Most people don't understand the fundamental strategies involved in making sound short-term investments.

21

A) NO CHANGE

B) dried

C) had dried

D) has dried

22

A) NO CHANGE

B) keeping

C) keep

D) make sure that you keep

Questions 23-33 are based on the following passage.

Aspiring to a Spire: Domfront's New Church

To most people, the phrase "country village in France" instantly conjures up the **23** image of a group of houses in the middle of verdant pasture, or nestled in the protective curve of rolling hills, or perched on the peak of a stony outcrop. There will be a bakery for warm fresh baguettes, a small, low-roofed café with its parasol tables where **24** urbanites from Paris scoff at this provincial life. There will be a war memorial, and a church, the bells of which will chime the day away.

Domfront, where I live in Lower Normandy, has all these features with one omission: the central church. Established in the early Middle Ages, Domfront does not seem to have had much success with religious structures, despite the fact that the town **25** lie on the pilgrimage road from Paris to the Abbey of Saint Michel on the coast. In the beginning, there were three Gothic churches here; all are now picturesque ruins **26** currently.

[1] In modern times, the village's efforts centered on Saint Julien's plaza, where the small Chapel of Saint Julien once stood. [2] This chapel was **27** raised in the eighteenth century and rebuilt fifty yards away on a wider area. [3] The townspeople should not have **28** bothered, without the enlarged and reconstructed edifice fell into a state of near-collapse by the end of the nineteenth century. [4] Yet Domfront decided to approach the Church of Saint Julien anew after World War I. [5] The resurrected structure would be distinguished by its

23
A) NO CHANGE
B) image with
C) image that
D) images in which

24
Which choice provides the most relevant detail?
A) NO CHANGE
B) the villagers smoke and chat and read their newspapers.
C) the townsfolk discuss the gentrification of their rural existence.
D) tourists find respite from a long day of sightseeing.

25
A) NO CHANGE
B) lay
C) lays
D) lies

26
A) NO CHANGE
B) today
C) presently
D) DELETE the underlined portion

27
A) NO CHANGE
B) risen
C) razing
D) razed

28
A) NO CHANGE
B) bothered, since
C) bothered, but
D) bothered for,

CONTINUE

neo-Byzantine design: the church would be built not in the traditional shape of a Latin cross, [29] but the square shape characteristic of Byzantine churches, a much more space-efficient layout. [6] To cut down the cost, the planners also decided to build the church using concrete, not cut stone. [7] Nonetheless, Domfront has persisted in [30] it's church-building. [31]

It took nineteen years to complete the building [32] (in part because the planners decided to add a fifty-one meter spire after the central dome was already built). Domfront's Church of Saint Julien consequently became a prominent part of the local scenery, easily seen from miles away. However, in the end, the weight of the spire was punishing to the concrete supports. The church had to be closed for safety reasons in the 1990s, just seventy years after it was completed.

Yet all was not lost. In 2013, Domfront completed a final round of repairs and the bells of Saint Julien [33] rung once more. The Domfront citizenry was ecstatic! The local pastry shop created special cakes for the occasion, and the local café hosted light festivities. If history is kind, the church will last forever.

29
A) NO CHANGE
B) but also
C) but in
D) but even

30
A) NO CHANGE
B) its
C) its'
D) their

31
To make this paragraph most logical, sentence 7 should be placed
A) where it is now.
B) before sentence 1.
C) before sentence 4.
D) before sentence 6.

32
The writer is considering deleting the parenthetical statement. Should the writer do so?
A) Yes, because it does not provide a specific example.
B) Yes, because it distracts from the main idea of the sentence.
C) No, because it provides additional detail supporting the main idea of the sentence.
D) No, because it continues the description of Byzantine architecture begun in the previous paragraph.

33
A) NO CHANGE
B) rang
C) rings
D) will ring

Questions 34-44 are based on the following passage.

Giving Your Two Scents

The British poet and novelist Rudyard Kipling wrote that "scents are surer than sights or sounds/ To make the heart strings crack." He intuitively understood what modern science and commerce have demonstrated: scents can trigger powerful psychological associations. Tastes are equally compelling. **34** Despite this, it is obvious that different flavors will drive consumer preferences for products such as food and beverages, flavor is also crucial to a growing number of non-edible goods, from dental floss to lipstick.

[1] The power of flavor and fragrance to influence consumer experiences **35** drive a global industry worldwide. [2] In the nineteenth century, it gradually became possible to synthesize aroma chemicals, allowing for the reproduction of characteristic tastes and smells. [3] Consumer goods associated with the flavor and fragrance industry now include pet food, vitamins, and laundry detergent, not to mention food, beverages, and perfumes. [4] Among these sensation-oriented products, which grow ever more varied, exotic and complex combinations of scents and tastes **36** has become increasingly more commoner. [5] Since then, more and more products have begun to appear in scented or flavored varieties. **37**

34
A) NO CHANGE
B) While
C) Given that
D) DELETE the underlined portion and begin the sentence with a capital letter.

35
A) NO CHANGE
B) drives a global industry worldwide.
C) drive a global industry.
D) drives a global industry.

36
A) NO CHANGE
B) have become increasingly more common
C) has become increasingly commoner
D) have become increasingly common

37
To make this paragraph most logical, sentence 5 should be placed
A) where it is now.
B) after sentence 1.
C) after sentence 2.
D) after sentence 3.

CONTINUE

Flavor and fragrance are usually only small components of a finished product, typically accounting for between one and five percent of manufacturing attention, yet consumers will often [38] cite taste or smell as a top reason for preferring one brand [39] against another. The fragrance and flavor industry thus [40] occupying a position at the intersection of psychology and [41] science, it relies on a highly sophisticated set of processes to accurately reproduce and combine scents and flavors, and on an understanding of what individuals find appealing about certain smells and tastes. It is also both global and culture-specific: there will be very different expectations of what might smell "fresh" or "cozy" in different regions of the world. The complexity of the industry means that the jobs within it are wide-ranging and rely on different skill sets. While chemists perform the technical work of synthesizing flavor and fragrance compounds, focus group coordinators test how consumers are likely to respond to new combinations and marketing specialists develop strategies for branding and promotion.

38
A) NO CHANGE
B) site taste
C) sight taste
D) siting taste

39
A) NO CHANGE
B) than
C) to
D) at

40
A) NO CHANGE
B) occupies
C) occupy
D) occupy's

41
A) NO CHANGE
B) science: it relies
C) science; which relies
D) science, they rely

The flavor and fragrance business [42] were experiencing steady growth since 2011 and is projected to continue to grow at least through 2017. The global sector of this industry is now estimated to have [43] an annual value of 25 billion dollars each year. [44] The reasons for steady growth include the constant consumption of scented and flavored products; for example, laundry detergent is used every time clothes are washed. Expenditures on these products also tend to vary relatively little during periods of economic fluctuation. For as long as the prospect of a pleasant scent or delicious taste can entice consumers, the market for flavor and fragrance is likely to thrive.

[42]
A) NO CHANGE
B) have experienced
C) has experienced
D) had experienced

[43]
A) NO CHANGE
B) an annual yearly value of 25 billion dollars.
C) an annual value of 25 billion dollars per year.
D) an annual value of 25 billion dollars.

[44]
A) NO CHANGE
B) Huge things about
C) Big causes behind
D) Main things leading up to

STOP
If you finish before time is called, you may check your work on this section only.
Do not turn to any other section.

No Test Material On This Page

Answer Key: TEST 3

Test 3

READING: SECTION 1

PASSAGE 1
Fiction

1. D
2. B
3. C
4. C
5. B
6. D
7. D
8. C
9. D
10. A

PASSAGE 2
Social Science

11. B
12. D
13. B
14. C
15. A
16. D
17. A
18. B
19. D
20. C

PASSAGE 3
Natural Science 1

21. C
22. D
23. A
24. A
25. C
26. A
27. C
28. B
29. B
30. D
31. B

PASSAGE 4
Global Conversation

32. C
33. A
34. C
35. C
36. A
37. B
38. B
39. C
40. B
41. A
42. A

PASSAGE 5
Natural Science 2

43. C
44. A
45. B
46. D
47. D
48. A
49. B
50. C
51. A
52. A

GRAMMAR: SECTION 2

PASSAGE 1
Mutual Attraction: New Magnetic Metals

1. A
2. D
3. B
4. C
5. B
6. B
7. A
8. B
9. C
10. D
11. B

PASSAGE 2
More Than One Way to Bounce a Dead Cat

12. B
13. D
14. A
15. C
16. D
17. C
18. B
19. A
20. B
21. D
22. C

PASSAGE 3
Aspiring to a Spire: Domfront's New Church

23. A
24. B
25. D
26. D
27. D
28. B
29. C
30. B
31. B
32. C
33. B

PASSAGE 4
Giving Your Two Scents

34. B
35. D
36. D
37. C
38. A
39. C
40. B
41. B
42. C
43. D
44. A

Once you have determined how many questions you answered correctly, consult the chart on Page 156 to determine **your scaled SAT Verbal score.**

Please visit **ies2400.com/answers** for answer explanations.

Post-Test Analysis

This post-test analysis is essential if you want to see an improvement on your next test. Possible reasons for errors on the Reading and Grammar passages in this test are listed here. Place check marks next to the types of errors that pertain to you, or write your own types of errors in the blank spaces.

TIMING AND ACCURACY

◇ Spent too long reading individual passages
◇ Spent too long answering each question
◇ Spent too long on a few difficult questions
◇ Felt rushed and made silly mistakes or random errors
◇ Unable to work quickly using error types and POE
Other: _____

APPROACHING THE PASSAGES AND QUESTIONS

◇ Unable to effectively grasp a passage's tone or style
◇ Unable to effectively grasp a passage's topic or stance
◇ Did not understand the context of line references or underlined portions
◇ Did not eliminate false answers using strong evidence
◇ Answered questions using first impressions instead of POE
◇ Answered questions without checking or inserting final answer
◇ Eliminated correct answer during POE
Other: _____

> **Use this form** to better analyze your performance. If you don't understand why you made errors, there is no way that you can correct them!

READING TEST: # CORRECT_____ # WRONG _____ # OMITTED _____

◇ Interpreted passages rather than working with evidence
◇ Used outside knowledge rather than working with evidence
◇ Unable to effectively identify a passage's purpose or argument
◇ Unable to work effectively with word in context questions
◇ Unable to work effectively with questions about structure and writing technique
◇ Unable to work accurately or efficiently with Command of Evidence questions
◇ Unable to draw logical conclusions based on the content of the passages
◇ Difficulties understanding graphics and relating them to the passages
Other: _____

GRAMMAR TEST: # CORRECT_____ # WRONG _____ # OMITTED _____

◇ Did not identify proper verb number, form, or tense
◇ Did identify proper pronoun agreement or pronoun form (subject/object, who/which/where)
◇ Did not test for proper comparison phrasing (amount/number, between/among)
◇ Did not test phrase for correct adverb/adjective usage
◇ Did not see broader sentence structure (parallelism, misplaced modifier)
◇ Did not see flaws in punctuation (colon, semicolon, comma splice, misplaced commas)
◇ Did not see tricky possessives or contractions (its/it's, your/you're)
◇ Did not identify flaws in standard phrases (either . . . or, not only . . . but also, etc.)
◇ Did not use proper phrasing in sentences requiring the subjunctive
◇ Did not notice wordiness, redundancy, or faulty idioms
◇ Did not notice excessively informal expressions or flaws in essay style
◇ Created the wrong relationship between two sentences or two paragraphs
◇ Created the wrong placement for an out-of-order paragraph
◇ Did not properly read or analyze an insertion/deletion question
◇ Did not properly read or analyze the information in a graphic
◇ Understood a graphic, but could not identify the correct passage content
Other: _____

Test4

Reading Test

65 MINUTES, 52 QUESTIONS

Turn to Section 1 of your answer sheet to answer the questions in this section.

Each passage or pair of passages below is followed by a number of questions. After reading each passage or pair, choose the best answer to each question based on what is stated or implied in the passage or passages and in any accompanying graphics (such as a table or graph).

Questions 1-10 are based on the following passage.

This passage is taken from a humorous short story written early in the twenty-first century.

It's another April day with intermittent heavy showers. "Good for the garden!" says my neighbor, and yes, I can see that the plants I had carefully installed in the front last week are
Line making some effort to emerge. The clematis in the pot by the
5 front door has survived the winter and is growing rampantly, although the clematis against the wooden fence merely displays a few timid green shoots. The apple tree is beginning to show buds here and there, but it still looks hesitant, and there is no sign that a single one of the bulbs I planted in autumn is making an
10 effort to push through. I sigh. I am a terrible gardener, really: all enthusiasm and no patience. I wonder if whoever moves into this house after I leave will keep the garden going.

My reverie is interrupted by the arrival of a white van, which double-parks outside my gate. On the vehicle's side are
15 painted the words: "Mr. Dutton, Removals and Storage." I look at my watch. Mr. Dutton has arrived only an hour late. Mr. Dutton gets out of his van and walks up the path. He is a rather stocky man. His hair is cropped close to his skull and he sports a small earring in his left ear. He wears heavy boots, a sagging
20 pair of jeans, and a heavy belt, which is partially obscured by his overhanging belly. His T-shirt is emblazoned with a motorcycle logo and he also dons an open, ill-fitting jacket with leather shoulder pads. The fingers of his right hand vigorously work his mobile phone. He pauses at the gate, pockets his phone, grins
25 broadly at me, and approaches the door with the air of a busy executive. I invite him in and show him the items that I need to send into storage; we then sit down in the front room while Mr. Dutton works out the estimated price for the job, all the while pursuing a monologue that requires few interventions on my

30 behalf.

Mr. Dutton tells me that he understands that I am moving to Oregon, which is funny because he had an uncle who lived there. This uncle joined the Peace Corps over twenty years ago: Mr. Dutton hasn't heard from him since. Mr. Dutton then
35 informs me that he is paying top taxes in this country and that by the end of 2012 there will be an economic black hole because everyone paying top taxes will have moved elsewhere—as they are already doing. I try to work this logic out, but by the time I have, Mr. Dutton has moved on to his interest in pre-
40 Roman history. Do I realize that every thousand years, the earth suffers a cataclysmic disaster, as in 535 A.D. when Krakatoa exploded? (The actual date had escaped me.) It caused darkness for twenty years, and crop growth became minimal. And that affected societies all over the world: the Ming Dynasty in
45 China collapsed, as did the Aztec Empire in Mexico. If that were to happen today, this country would be finished. (I nod in agreement.) We would turn to cannibalism, since we import all our food. We would not know what to do, although, of course, the answer resides in one word: N.A.S.A. According to Mr.
50 Dutton, the U.N. should force everyone in the world to give up 5% of what they earn in order to finance spaceships, which would bring about the colonization of both Mars and the Moon. That, he says, is the future, and the quotation for storage for one year will be $1735.25. Will I be paying in advance?

55 With that, Mr. Dutton takes his leave, telling me just before he goes that MTV is a brilliant channel, since its costumes and music give young people the opportunity to learn about the world, and that it has been a pleasure to meet me, for I am clearly someone with a view to the future. More people like us,
60 he apparently feels, are needed if we are to survive the present difficulties. I see him to the front door, and watch him take out his mobile phone, enter his car, and roar off. I look once more at the garden, shrug my shoulders, and go back indoors.

CONTINUE ➡

1

It can be inferred that the author of the passage is

A) deeply enraged by the digressions of Mr Dutton.

B) enthralled by the idiosyncratic yet prudent ideals of Mr. Dutton.

C) slightly disoriented by Mr. Dutton's loquacity.

D) vexed by Mr. Dutton's unsavory political opinions.

2

As used in line 29, "pursuing" most nearly means

A) chasing.

B) conducting.

C) seeking.

D) scrutinizing.

3

Mr. Dutton's view on current affairs can best be described as

A) alarmist in its conclusions and somewhat sketchy in its evidence.

B) sanguine in its short term projections but ultimately pessimistic.

C) cautious in logical method and conservative in outlook.

D) politically brash but informed by extensive education in economics.

4

Which choice provides the best evidence for the answer to the previous question?

A) Lines 24-26 ("He pauses . . . executive")

B) Lines 40-43 ("Do I . . . minimal")

C) Lines 45-48 ("If that . . . food")

D) Lines 55-58 ("With that . . . the world")

5

The narrator describes Mr. Dutton in lines 13-26 ("My reverie . . . executive") in order to

A) portray the singular nature of Mr. Dutton's appearance and mannerisms.

B) attempt to put out of mind the ill treatment the garden has suffered as the result of negligence.

C) emphasize the narrator's own lack of a cultivated and sophisticated countenance.

D) suggest that Mr. Dutton is too distracted by his mobile phone to perform his job adequately.

6

The question in line 54 ("Will I be paying in advance?") can best be characterized as

A) worried.

B) angered.

C) ironic.

D) thoughtful.

7

According to Mr. Dutton, the solution to the dire state of the world's future can best be found in

A) gardening.

B) hard work.

C) tax reform.

D) space exploration.

8

As used in line 56, "brilliant" most nearly means

A) blinding.

B) elite.

C) valuable.

D) knowledgeable.

9

It can be inferred from the passage that Mr. Dutton thinks of the narrator as

A) an unconcerned individual who has little to say about the important matters facing society.

B) a dependable ally in desperate times.

C) a shrewd yet eloquent adversary.

D) a devoted friend who can adapt to changing social circumstances.

10

Which choice provides the best evidence for the answer to the previous question?

A) Lines 24-30 ("He pauses . . . behalf")

B) Lines 38-40 ("I try . . . history")

C) Lines 48-52 ("We would not . . . Moon")

D) Lines 58-61 ("it has been . . . difficulties")

Questions 11-20 are based on the following passages.

How do societies change as they become increasingly large and complex? In these readings, two authors consider this issue from different perspectives.

Passage 1

Complexity kills. You should know this well if you have ever tried to develop a long, intricate argument, only to find that everyone has stopped paying attention to you a tenth of

Line the way through. But there are times in history when, quite

5 literally, complexity has exerted a lethal influence. As a society grows larger, it necessarily develops new capacities to meet new challenges, yet in so doing expands and expands until its basic operations are no longer sustainable.

This is exactly the argument that was laid out in *The*

10 *Collapse of Complex Societies* by Joseph Tainter, a book that first appeared in 1988 and that continues to be a house favorite among sociology and anthropology buffs. Among the societies that Tainter has considered are some of the most remarkable the world has seen, including the Romans

15 and the Mayas. To demonstrate how these societies failed, Tainter marshals concepts from classic economic and political theory: an aggressively expanding society would inevitably decentralize, stretch, and weaken, since the costs of expanding would eventually outstrip the benefits to be gained from such

20 expansion. Such an attenuated society would then be forced (often to its detriment) to rely on new allies, or would be forced (certainly to its detriment) to accumulate crippling debts. There is much that Tainter's theory explains, yet there is also much about sociology and anthropology that has changed since

25 1988. Tainter has little interest in genuinely small societies with primitive technologies. He also neglects the very forces— including ideological and religious bonds—that can hold even a dying society together for an astonishingly long period of time. These considerations make sociological ideas of complexity

30 more unruly, more unpredictable, and indeed more complex. Do ideologically-centralized societies exhibit healthy growth, or are they little more than eventual victims of the complexity that kills?

Passage 2

What is it that makes a society grow larger and more

35 complex? A recent study put forth by Joseph Watts, an anthropology student at the University of Auckland, presents an interesting hypothesis. Apparently, the development of small-scale communities into large chiefdoms and city-states hinges upon the nature of the religious beliefs of the general populace.

40 After studying 96 different cultures spread across Australia and Indonesia, Watts found a correlation between the belief in deities that are capable of punishing selfish behavior and the development of relatively large and complex societies. The

reason for this, argues Watts, is that in smaller communities,

45 everyone knows everyone else, and people tend to behave and abide by the rules because friends and family are always watching; to transgress would be to lose one's reputation. As societies grow larger, however, crime becomes more of a problem: it is much easier to steal from someone you don't know

50 than from someone you have to see each day.

According to Watts, this is where the belief in punishing deities becomes a kind of "glue" that keeps a society together. The punishing god functions as a kind of invisible cop in the sky watching and making sure no one breaks the rules. Fewer rules

55 are disobeyed and the society prospers.

This is certainly an interesting theory, and Watts' recent study seems to confirm it. Among the 96 tribes studied, thirty-seven held beliefs in supernatural deities capable of punishing selfish acts, such as shirking a sacrifice or flouting a taboo.

60 The statistics also suggest that belief in such gods predates the development of societies with greater political complexity. If Watts' theory proves true, it may replace older modes of thought which held that an all-powerful, moralizing deity was the impetus for a more complex society. The truth, however, may lie

65 with the "small gods," not with the big ones.

11

It can be inferred that the author of Passage 1 believes that complexity

A) is inevitably destructive to large civilizations.

B) can weaken but never completely destroy a prosperous civilization.

C) should be produced through decentralized governance and local reforms.

D) may not be explained by a single unified theory.

12

Which choice provides the best evidence for the answer to the previous question?

A) Lines 4-5 ("But there . . . influence")

B) Lines 12-15 ("Among the . . . Mayas")

C) Lines 25-26 ("Tainter has . . . technologies")

D) Lines 29-30 ("These considerations . . . complex")

CONTINUE

13

According to Joseph Tainter, complex societies tend to collapse because

A) they are often easy targets for foreign invasion or internal rebellion.

B) too much is spent and not enough gained in the process of political expansion.

C) they are often spread out to such an extent that a single identity is no longer feasible.

D) they lack the trust and emotional bonds present within small societies.

14

The author of Passage 1 refers back to the publication date (in line 25) of Tainter's book in order to

A) emphasize how outdated Tainter's archaeological information is.

B) observe that Tainter's breakthrough in anthropology was relatively recent.

C) transition from a description to a critique of Tainter's theory.

D) argue that new cases of collapsed societies since 1988 necessitate revisions to Tainter's argument.

15

As used in line 16, "marshals" most nearly means

A) commands.

B) arranges.

C) disciplines.

D) utilizes.

16

The references to "glue" (line 52) and the "cop in the sky" (line 53) serve to indicate how

A) the threat of divine retribution can keep a society functioning.

B) the belief in supernatural powers can inhibit scientific and technological advancement.

C) societies with strong religious convictions tend to revere and preserve their natural surroundings.

D) Western anthropologists still have incomplete ideas about the role of myth and belief in primitive societies.

17

The last paragraph of Passage 2 suggests that the development of a "moralizing deity" (line 63) is important primarily because this development

A) can cripple certain tribes while assisting others.

B) is instrumental in the transformation of large rural societies into urban civilizations.

C) was believed to be a precondition for creating a complex society out of small tribes.

D) is impossible without the religious institutions provided by large and complex societies.

18

Which describes the overall relationship between Passage 1 and Passage 2?

A) Passage 1 endorses a theory about a phenomenon, while Passage 2 expresses reservations about that theory.

B) Passage 1 critiques a theory about a phenomenon, while Passage 2 investigates the causes of that phenomenon.

C) Passage 1 presents and then disproves an argument, while Passage 2 defends some of the argument's assumptions.

D) Passage 1 takes issue with a methodology and Passage 2 uses a separate methodology to arrive at a similar conclusion.

19

How would the author of Passage 1 most likely respond to the theory set forward by Joseph Watts in Passage 2?

A) Complex societies would not need punishing deities if they were capable of maintaining functional civil institutions.

B) The development of punishing deities among small tribes will most likely lead to the destruction of those tribes.

C) Shared belief in punishing gods might keep even otherwise declining societies from collapse.

D) Unifying religious convictions enable a small tribal society to organize into a large empire.

20

Which choice provides the best evidence for the answer to the previous question?

A) Lines 5-8 ("As a society. . . sustainable")

B) Lines 17-20 ("an aggressively . . . expansion")

C) Lines 20-22 ("Such an . . . debts")

D) Lines 26-28 ("He also . . . of time")

Questions 21-30 are based on the following passage and supplementary material.

The passage below is taken from a 2014 essay that considers the possibility of sympathy between humanity and different animal species.

David Blunkett is a member of the British Parliament, one who is held in particular affection by the general public. The reason for this is two-fold. First, he has been blind since
Line childhood, yet has not been prevented from holding high
5 office. Second, he is always seen on television and in public accompanied by his guide dog. There have been six in his life so far, most of which have sat through noisy sessions in the House of Commons, apparently indifferent to the hubbub surrounding Blunkett, concerned only with the role of devoted guide and
10 guard.
    Blunkett is retiring from Parliament this year, and he has been writing about the relationship between his dogs and himself; it is his conviction that dogs have a remarkable ability to read and understand the emotions of humans. For him, dogs can
15 interpret the body language of their owners and react with the same caring responses that humans often direct at one another: soothing, gently correcting, sometimes cautioning gestures. Inspiring though this conception is, it is a conception with a complex history.
20   It is believed that the dog has existed in its present forms for at least eleven thousand years, although some experts would suggest that the dog appeared even before that, perhaps as early as sixteen thousand years ago. Yet it is generally accepted that the dog we know today has its ancestral roots in a wolf
25 species—not the common European grey wolf, but a now-extinct earlier wolf population. Charles Darwin, in his definitive work *The Origin of Species*, could only conclude that the domestic dog may be descended from more than one wild ancestor. The same, perhaps, is the case for kindred species such as the Arctic
30 Wolf, the Red Fox, and the Coyote. It is generally assumed that, like these distant cousins of today's dogs, the original

dog was a "hunter gatherer" species, one that formed packs to harass its prey. However, none of these natural "relations" really anticipates the bond of domesticity. Very rarely do "hunter
35 gatherer" animals cooperate with alien species—and almost never to the extent that the dog has cooperated with human beings.
    In his article "How Dog Became the Dog," American journalist Mark Derr suggests that the dog could only have
40 developed its present relationship with humans as a result of "attentiveness, curiosity, necessity, and recognition of the advantage gained through collaboration." At first glance, Derr's conclusion might seem to be relatively logical, though the more deeply his logic is considered, the more disturbing
45 it becomes. Perhaps a dog's sympathetic ability to recognize human emotion is not a special "ability" at all, just evolutionary common sense—an essential means of separating encouraging and threatening stimuli. However, what would be common sense in the dog's original, uncertain natural environment should not
50 be misread when it is displayed elsewhere. One consequence of Derr's idea that the dog recognizes "the advantage gained though collaboration" is that dogs may be better manipulators than we think. They put on shows of devotion to secure survival, knowing that humans value these apparent reactions, but perhaps
55 not feeling anything like the emotions we humans feel.
    Whatever the cause of a dog's actions may be, we have to accept that many people are prone to attribute all kinds of intelligence and sensitivity to dogs. Why wonder? A dog is a cheerful companion, especially if one lives alone, and can ignite
60 an innately human sense of responsibility. What is revealed by such a relationship tells us more about the fallibility and sentimentality of humans than about the ulterior motives of dogs. For example, many people are as convinced as David Blunkett is that dogs share our ideas of anger and sorrow. Others declare that
65 a dog will defend the person with whom it lives. (Disgruntled postmen can certainly attest to this.) Yet perhaps the motivations can be disregarded, when dogs and humans are both the better for their bonds.

The following graph indicates the average response for guide dogs in the Guide Dogs of America training sequence. These dogs responded either successfully or unsuccessfully with the associated trained response to the trainer's various human gestures.

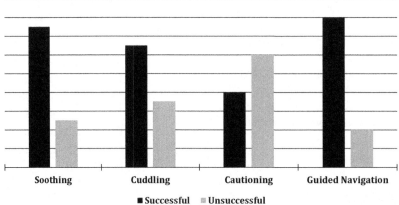

Guide Dog Responses to Human Gestures (Training)

Soothing   Cuddling   Cautioning   Guided Navigation
■ Successful   ▪ Unsuccessful

CONTINUE

21

What function does the third paragraph serve in the passage as a whole?

A) To shed doubt on David Blunkett's theory

B) To underscore the characterization of dogs as docile

C) To discuss the inconclusive ancestry of the dog

D) To introduce Mark Derr's ideas and theories

22

Which choice does the author explicitly cite as a possible advantage of the bond between dogs and humans?

A) Dogs can help humans to understand and communicate strong emotions.

B) Dogs are easily trained to perform simple tasks.

C) Dogs offer their owners practical assistance and protection.

D) Dogs readily sympathize with handicapped people.

23

Which choice provides the best evidence for the answer to the previous questions?

A) Lines 6-10 ("There have . . . guard")

B) Lines 34-35 ("Very rarely . . . alien species")

C) Lines 53-54 ("They put on . . . reactions")

D) Lines 66-68 ("Yet perhaps . . . bonds")

24

One of the central assumptions of the passage is that

A) dogs are motivated solely by the need for food.

B) dogs are motivated by emotion, not by logic.

C) the dog's original environment required cooperation with other animal species

D) dogs may be more opportunistic than they are popularly believed to be.

25

Which choice provides the best evidence for the answer to the previous question?

A) Lines 45-48 ("Perhaps a . . . stimuli")

B) Lines 48-50 ("However . . . elsewhere")

C) Lines 50-53 ("One consequence . . . we think")

D) Lines 58-60 ("A dog . . . responsibility")

26

As used in line 34, "anticipates" most nearly means

A) explains.

B) expects.

C) predicts.

D) considers.

27

In the final paragraph, the author refers to "many people" in order to

A) indicate the growing popularity of Mark Derr's ideas.

B) underscore the prevalence of possible misconceptions about dogs.

C) highlight a development that weakens David Blunkett's claims.

D) resolve a debate about the motives of dogs.

28

As used in line 49, "uncertain" most nearly means

A) unusual.

B) unknown.

C) dangerous.

D) intriguing.

29

Based on the passage and the graph, which of the following guide dog responses would the author cite as contradictory to Blunkett's claims?

A) Soothing

B) Cuddling

C) Cautioning

D) Guided Navigation

30

Which choice is best supported by the information in the graph?

A) Trained dogs and humans share an inherent sympathetic bond.

B) Human trainers failed to provide appropriate gestures to elicit the cautioning response.

C) Guide dogs are most successful overall in guided navigation.

D) Disciplined dogs only react with sympathy to non-threatening human gestures.

CONTINUE   107

Questions 31-41 are based on the following passage.

This consideration of American enterprise is an excerpt from *Random Reminiscences of Men and Events* (1909), the memoir of businessman John D. Rockefeller.

I confess I have no sympathy with the idea so often advanced that our basis of all judgments in this country is founded on money. If this were true, we should be a nation
Line of money hoarders instead of spenders. Nor do I admit that
5 we are so small-minded a people as to be jealous of the success of others. It is the other way about: we are the most extraordinarily ambitious, and the success of one man in any walk of life spurs the others on. It does not sour them, and it is a libel even to suggest so great a meanness of spirit.
10 In reading the newspapers, where so much is taken for granted in considering things on a money standard, I think we need some of the sense of humor possessed by an Irish neighbor of mine, who built what we regarded as an extremely ugly house, which stood out in bright colors as we looked
15 from our windows. My taste in architecture differed so widely from that affected by my Irish friend, that we planted out the view of his house by moving some large trees to the end of our property. Another neighbor who watched this work going on asked Mr. Foley why Mr. Rockefeller moved all these big trees
20 and cut off the view between the houses. Foley, with the quick wit of his country, responded instantly: "It's invy, they can't stand looking at the ividence of me prosperity."
In my early days men acted just as they do now, no doubt. When there was anything to be done for general trade
25 betterment, almost every man had some good reason for believing that his case was a special one different from all the rest. For every foolish thing he did, or wanted to do, for every unbusiness-like plan he had, he always pleaded that it was necessary in his case. He was the one man who had to
30 sell at less than cost, to disrupt all the business plans of others in his trade, because his individual position was so absolutely different from all the rest. It was often a heart-breaking undertaking to convince those men that the perfect occasion which would lead to the perfect opportunity would never come,
35 even if they waited until the crack o' doom.
Then, again, we had the type of man who really never knew all the facts about his own affairs. Many of the brightest kept their books in such a way that they did not actually know when they were making money on a certain operation and
40 when they were losing. This unintelligent competition was a hard matter to contend with. Good old-fashioned common sense has always been a mighty rare commodity. When a man's affairs are not going well, he hates to study the books and face the truth. From the first, the men who managed the Standard
45 Oil Company kept their books intelligently as well as correctly. We knew how much we made and where we gained or lost. At least, we tried not to deceive ourselves.

My ideas of business are no doubt old-fashioned, but the fundamental principles do not change from generation
50 to generation, and sometimes I think that our quick-witted American business men, whose spirit and energy are so splendid, do not always sufficiently study the real underlying foundations of business management. I have spoken of the necessity of being frank and honest with oneself about one's
55 own affairs: many people assume that they can get away from the truth by avoiding thinking about it, but the natural law is inevitable, and the sooner it is recognized, the better.
One hears a great deal about wages and why they must be maintained at a high level, by the railroads, for example. A
60 laborer is worthy of his hire, no less, but no more, and in the long run he must contribute an equivalent for what he is paid.

31

According to Rockefeller, the "men" in line 44
A) were fully aware of their company's finances.
B) struggled to keep the Standard Oil Company open.
C) were initially skeptical of John D. Rockefeller's business practices.
D) were young and vivacious opportunity-seekers.

32

The primary purpose of the first paragraph is to establish that
A) John D. Rockefeller struggles to feel compassion for poor businessmen.
B) some people make defamatory claims about the United States.
C) the success of others generates ambition, not jealousy.
D) people should spend money rather than save it.

33

As used in line 2, "advanced" most nearly means
A) proposed.
B) learned.
C) improved.
D) evolved.

CONTINUE

34

John D. Rockefeller describes himself as "old-fashioned" primarily because he

A) is older and more experienced than other businessmen.

B) realizes that he is not modernizing along with the rest of his industry.

C) does not value what younger men value.

D) believes that the basics of enterprise are immutable.

35

The third paragraph (lines 23-35) is concerned with establishing a contrast between

A) self-absorption and pragmatism.

B) malice and generosity.

C) privacy and publicity.

D) current problems and possible reforms.

36

The example in the last paragraph primarily serves to

A) advocate for fair wages across the transportation industry.

B) illustrate a basic tenet of sound business management.

C) introduce the concept of business ethics.

D) suggest that it is difficult to put a monetary value on labor.

37

It can most reasonably be inferred that Rockefeller differs from other American businessmen because he

A) unavoidably feels envious of others' success.

B) appreciates the need to accurately assess his business.

C) values acquiring land over maintaining neighborly relationships.

D) finds humor in difficult business situations.

38

Which choice provides the best evidence for the answer to the previous question?

A) Lines 1-3 ("I confess . . . money")

B) Lines 15-16 ("My taste . . . friend")

C) Lines 41-42 ("Good . . . commodity")

D) Lines 53-55 ("I have . . . affairs")

39

According to the passage, John D. Rockefeller would most likely agree that

A) Mr. Foley often acts unreasonably during discussions about architecture.

B) American businessmen are sensible but neither clever nor witty.

C) some businessmen selfishly introduce disorder into other businesses.

D) the men of the past were more rational than Rockefeller's contemporaries in America.

40

Which choice provides the best evidence for the answer to the previous question?

A) Lines 8-9 ("It does . . . spirit")

B) Lines 29-32 ("He was . . . the rest")

C) Lines 36-37 ("Then . . . affairs")

D) Lines 46-47 ("At least . . . ourselves")

41

As used in line 20, "cut off" most nearly means

A) shortened.

B) bypassed.

C) obstructed.

D) silenced.

CONTINUE ➔

Questions 42-52 are based on the following passage and supplementary material.

The following passage was written by a specialist in inorganic chemistry

Down at the bottom of the periodic table lie the lesser-known elements: halfnium, seaborgium, meitnerium, and many other obscurities that are not discussed in any introductory
Line chemistry course. There is a reason for this. Due to their
5 extremely heavy nuclei, these elements are highly unstable, and they undergo spontaneous radioactive decay into smaller, more stable atoms. Some of these elements' half-lives are mere fractions of seconds; they don't even stick around long enough for us to glimpse them, and we recognize them only from the
10 decay particles they leave behind. For scientists hunting for new elements, the search is akin to analyzing a fissure left in the clouds by the speeding blur of a supersonic jet.

This may all be changing. For years, scientists have speculated that out beyond the unstable heavy elements,
15 there may lie an "island of stability"—a rare region in which superheavy elements, even heavier than those yet discovered, may finally achieve much longer half-lives than those yet observed. Many chemists working in the field have hypothesized a series of "magic numbers," combinations of protons and
20 neutrons that, if they could be brought together, might yield novel, stable nuclei. So far, the magic numbers include arrangements of 108, 110, and 114 protons, each combined with 184 neutrons. The reason for the speculated stability of such nuclei is that they would have the potential to form a structure
25 known as the "bubble configuration," in which the superheavy nucleus has a hole in its center. These nuclei "have never been discovered yet, but the region that is being explored right now is really on the edge of bubble territory," remarked Witold Nazarewicz of the Oak Ridge National Laboratory in Tennessee.
30 In nature, the heaviest element that occurs with any abundance is uranium, which contains only 92 protons. So how do scientists manage to create such superheavy nuclei? The answer, despite the advanced science involved, is something any layperson can understand, because it involves only simple arithmetic.
35 As anyone with decent mental math can tell you, the sum of 20 and 97 is 117. Recently, at the Joint Institute for Nuclear Research in Dubna, Russia, a team of American and Russian scientists took advantage of this fact by accelerating isotopes of calcium (which contain 20 protons) to 10 percent of the speed of
40 light. They then bombarded these calcium atoms against isotopes of berkelium (which contain 97 protons). On the rare occasions when the two nucleus types collided head-on, they fused together to briefly create a new nucleus that contained 117 protons; for a brief moment, a new element was born. Like all superheavy
45 nuclei, however, this nucleus quickly decayed. Nonetheless, even the decay particles of Element 117 were unique. One

of them was a never-before-seen isotope of lawrencium (103 protons, 163 neutrons), which exhibited a half-life of 11 hours—far longer and more stable than any of the half-lives observed
50 for previously examined isotopes of lawrencium. Physicist Christoph Dullman, who led the series of experiments, remarked, "Perhaps we are on the shore of the island of stability."

The discovery has important implications. If the island of stability does exist, new elements with highly stable half-lives—
55 perhaps as long as thousands to even millions of years—could be synthesized. It is also possible that such elements already exist in nature, but that they are so rare that they have yet to be discovered. Now that there is evidence that supports their possible existence, the search for the island of stability looks
60 more promising than ever. "All existing data for elements 116, 117, and 118 do confirm that lifetimes increase as one gets closer to the neutron number 184," said Nazarewicz. "This is encouraging."

Isotope Information

Isotope	Half-Life	Number of Protons
Calcium-47	4.5 days	20
Element-117	11 hours	117
Berkelium-245	4.94 days	97
Lawrencium-260	2.7 minutes	103

42

As used in line 6, "spontaneous" most nearly means

A) instinctual.
B) straightforward.
C) automatic.
D) impulsive.

43

The author uses the comparison in lines 10-12 ("For scientists . . . supersonic jet") in order to imply that some elements

A) move extremely fast.
B) disappear quickly.
C) are studied by engineers.
D) are unusually heavy.

CONTINUE ▶

44

According to the passage, the process of creating superheavy nuclei

A) is in some respects easy to comprehend.
B) requires equipment only available in Russia.
C) has yet to be discovered.
D) must be completed within 11 hours.

45

Which choice provides the best evidence for the answer to the previous question?

A) Lines 1-4 ("Down at . . . course")
B) Lines 13-15 ("For years . . . stability")
C) Lines 32-34 ("The answer . . . arithmetic")
D) Lines 41-43 ("On the . . . protons")

46

The author implies that superheavy, stable elements

A) cannot be synthesized in laboratory settings.
B) could occur outside controlled environments.
C) are believed to only exist in theory.
D) are solely of interest to atomic physicists.

47

Which choice provides the best evidence for the answer to the previous question?

A) Lines 4-7 ("Due to . . . atoms")
B) Lines 30-31 ("In nature . . . protons")
C) Lines 46-47 ("One of . . . lawrencium")
D) Lines 56-57 ("It is . . . nature")

48

The main purpose of the passage is to

A) outline the progress in the search for superheavy elements.
B) indicate the potential medical uses of superheavy elements.
C) imply that superheavy elements may exist in outer space.
D) garner public support for inorganic chemistry research.

49

As used in line 38, "accelerating" most nearly means

A) increasing.
B) speeding up.
C) growing.
D) enhancing.

50

According to the passage, the "bubble configuration" mentioned in line 25 is significant because it

A) allows superheavy elements to form the largest possible arrangements.
B) is arranged to include up to 184 protons.
C) provides stability for superheavy elements.
D) is the structure of several unstable elements listed in the periodic table.

51

Do the data in the table support Witold Nazarewicz's claim about "lifetimes" (line 61)?

A) Yes, because Element 117 has the highest number of protons.
B) Yes, because the number of protons is directly proportional to the half-life of the isotope.
C) No, because it fails to address the number of electrons necessary to support his claim.
D) No, because the table does not include the necessary information about neutron numbers.

52

It can be inferred from the data in the chart that

A) an isotope's half life is directly correlated to the isotope's nuclear mass.
B) an isotope's half life is directly correlated to the number of neutrons.
C) proton number does not correlate directly to an element's half-life.
D) the number of neutrons always exceeds the number of protons in super-heavy elements.

STOP

If you finish before time is called, you may check your work on this section only.
Do not turn to any other section.

Writing Test
35 MINUTES, 44 QUESTIONS

Turn to Section 2 of your answer sheet to answer the questions in this section.

DIRECTIONS

Each passage below is accompanied by a number of questions. For some questions, you will consider how the passage might be revised to improve the expression of ideas. For other questions, you will consider how the passage might be edited to correct errors in sentence structure, usage, or punctuation. A passage or a question may be accompanied by one or more graphics (such as a table or graph) that you will consider as you make revising and editing decisions.

Some questions will direct you to an underlined portion of a passage. Other questions will direct you to a location in a passage or ask you to think about the passage as a whole.

After reading each passage, choose the answer to each question that most effectively improves the quality of writing in the passage or that makes the passage conform to the conventions of standard written English. Many questions include a "NO CHANGE" option. Choose that option if you think the best choice is to leave the relevant portion of the passage as it is.

Questions 1-11 are based on the following passage.

The Digital Generation

Can you remember a world before the Internet? For many individuals born in the mid-1980s or later, the answer is no. "Digital natives" is a term that has been used to refer to people **1** that have lived the entirety of their lives surrounded by the digital technology that has come to define much of contemporary culture. Marc Prensky, an educational consultant, coined the term in 2001. The term was adapted from the notion of a "native speaker" of a **2** language, that is someone who was never formally "taught" a language but acquired it naturally through early exposure. Likewise, a whole generation has grown up in a world where computers, videos, video games, and social media are **3** all over the place. In contrast, older people are known as

1
A) NO CHANGE
B) who
C) whom
D) DELETE the underlined portion.

2
A) NO CHANGE
B) language that is
C) language that,
D) language:

3
A) NO CHANGE
B) universal.
C) commonplace.
D) invasive.

CONTINUE

"digital immigrants" **4** :these individuals have been introduced to digital tools and technologies later in life and have had to adapt.

Much of the interest in the notion of a generation of digital natives has involved questions of conflict **5** between this group and today's large population of digital immigrants. Education has often been a dominant issue. **6** Commentators who are friendly to digital natives argue that students now require the use of media and technology in classroom settings in order to learn effectively. However, many educators were never trained to incorporate technology. Educators may thus feel unsure about their competence. As a result, they may be perceived as increasingly **7** out of reach with the needs and expectations of a new generation of students.

4

The writer is considering deleting the underlined portion of the sentence. Should the writer do this?

A) Yes, because it repeats information already mentioned in the paragraph.

B) Yes, because it sets up a new topic at the end of the paragraph.

C) No, because it sets up the argument that older people lack direct experience with technology.

D) No, because it explains a term discussed earlier in the sentence.

5

A) NO CHANGE

B) between your

C) among this

D) amongst

6

Which choice most effectively combines the underlined sentences?

A) While commentators friendly to digital natives argue that students now require the use of media and technology in classroom settings in order to learn effectively, many educators were never trained to incorporate technology.

B) Commentators friendly to digital natives argue that students now require the use of media and technology in classroom settings in order to learn effectively; likewise, many educators were never trained to incorporate technology.

C) Contrasted with commentators friendly to digital natives arguing that students now require the use of media and technology in classroom settings in order to learn effectively, educators were never trained to incorporate technology.

D) When commentators friendly to digital natives argue that students now require the use of media and technology in classroom settings in order to learn effectively, many educators were never trained to incorporate technology.

7

A) NO CHANGE

B) out of touch

C) out of style

D) out of place

CONTINUE

Other conflicts between digital natives and those who acquired digital aptitudes later in life may arise in workplaces, **8** whereas increased reliance on technology and digital communication can put digital natives at an advantage and lead to tension with older staff members. Debates between parents and children **9** with reliance on and appropriate usage of cellphones, video games, and social media offer further examples of a potential gap in understanding.

[1] While recognizing and analyzing an apparent generational divide is valuable, **10** heavy reliance on the concept of the "digital native" risks oversimplification. [2] Not everyone born in the same era has had equal access to digital technologies. [3] Because access to technology is often tied to relatively high income and education, the digital native paradigm risks excluding individuals from certain socio-economic backgrounds. [4] Current research into digital media behaviors draws on a wide range of viewpoints. [5] This breadth of perspective is likely to provide an optimal understanding of how individuals have been affected by growing up in an electronic and online world. **11**

8
A) NO CHANGE
B) in which
C) where
D) from

9
A) NO CHANGE
B) in
C) on
D) about

10
A) NO CHANGE
B) being heavily relied
C) relying too heavily
D) heavy relying

11
Where is the most logical place in this paragraph to add the following sentence?

Thus individuals of the same age may differ radically in digital competence.

A) After sentence 1
B) After sentence 2
C) After sentence 3
D) After sentence 4

CONTINUE

Questions 12-22 are based on the following passage and supplementary material.

Cognitive Science Comes of Age

— 1 —

The set of mental processes through which the brain acquires knowledge [12] are known as cognitive functioning. These processes include perception, reasoning, problem solving, and the creation of memories. A number of [13] disruptions, such as strokes or head injuries, may lead these functions to become impaired. Individuals suffering from cognitive impairment may display problems recalling familiar information and may also find it difficult [14] completing simple tasks; they may also exhibit poor judgment or experience personality changes.

— 2 —

[15] In a world of rapidly expanding technology, medical professionals can employ any one of a number of different tests. These tests typically involve asking individuals to perform tasks related to one or more cognitive processes and then determining whether the individuals' abilities fall [16] to a normal range. [17] For example, in the Clock-Drawing Test, elderly patients will either be presented with a blank sheet of paper and be asked to draw a clock-face from memory, or be given a sheet with a circle printed on it and be asked to fill in the appropriate numbers. Some variations of the test will also require individuals to draw the hands of the clock positioned to indicate a specific time.

12
A) NO CHANGE
B) were
C) is
D) was

13
A) NO CHANGE
B) disruptions—such as strokes or head injuries,
C) disruptions such as strokes, or head injuries
D) disruptions such as, strokes or head injuries,

14
A) NO CHANGE
B) to complete
C) for the completion of
D) in completing

15
Which choice best introduces the paragraph?
A) NO CHANGE
B) As a testament to their ingenuity,
C) In order to identify cognitive impairment,
D) To find effective treatments for dementia,

16
A) NO CHANGE
B) for
C) throughout
D) within

17
A) NO CHANGE
B) Given that,
C) Finally,
D) To be clear,

— 3 —

Among the general population of today's advanced countries, aging is the primary cause of cognitive impairment. Cognitive impairment that significantly affects an elderly individual and disrupts 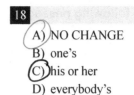 <u>their</u> daily life may be termed dementia, and the prevalence of dementia increases with age: a 2015 study suggests that 5% of individuals <u>aged 71 to 79 years experience dementia; for individuals aged 80 to 89 years, that figure rises to 68%.</u> Many other elderly individuals experience milder forms of cognitive impairment, which involve symptoms that are similar but not severe enough to indicate dementia.

18
- A) NO CHANGE
- B) one's
- C) his or her
- D) everybody's

19

Which choice offers the most accurate and relevant information from the data in the chart?
- A) NO CHANGE
- B) aged 71 to 79 years experience incontinence; for individuals aged 80 to 89 years, that figure rises to 22%.
- C) aged 71 to 79 years experience dementia; for individuals aged 80 to 89 years, that figure rises to 24%.
- D) aged 80 to 89 years experience dementia; for individuals aged 71 to 79 years, that figure rises to 41%.

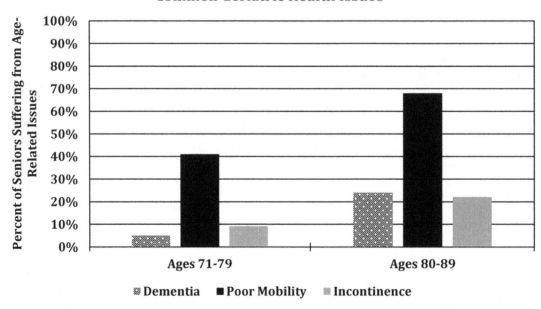

Common Geriatric Health Issues

CONTINUE

— 4 —

Despite the seeming lucidity of these procedures, various problems [20] are posed by the current methods of assessing cognitive functioning. There is the possibility of mis-diagnosis or inconclusive diagnosis, since uncontrollable factors that may lead to poor performance on a cognitive assessment test [21] can complicate test results. Conducting a full cognitive assessment is also often a lengthy process and requires a highly-trained supervisor, both to administer the assessment and to interpret and score the tests.

— 5 —

Fortunately, recent research has yielded cognitive assessment tools that are more accessible, such as brief questionnaires. The results of the questionnaires often require review by a physician, but these forms can offer a useful method for quickly identifying individuals likely to be suffering from cognitive impairment.

Question [22] asks about the previous passage as a whole.

20
A) NO CHANGE
B) is posed
C) posing
D) are being posed

21
The writer is considering adding the following information.

    —acute pain, chronic pain, and psychological distress (such as depression or anxiety)—

Should the writer make this addition here?
A) Yes, because it provides support for the writer's claim that many factors cause dementia.
B) Yes, because it elaborates on the writer's reference to uncontrollable factors.
C) No, because it would be better placed elsewhere in the passage.
D) No, because it provides detail that does not explain the main point of the paragraph.

Think about the previous passage as a whole as you answer question 22.

22
To make the passage most logical, paragraph 3 should be placed
A) where it is now.
B) after paragraph 1.
C) after paragraph 4.
D) after paragraph 5.

Questions 23-33 are based on the following passage.

The Rise and Fall of Vaudeville

Vaudeville, an American theatrical pastime, still exists today as the more commonly known "variety show." This form of theater began in the late 1800s and reached its peak popularity around 1910. In the early years of the twentieth century, Americans needed an escape from the unpleasant realities of urban crowding and menial labor. Audiences flocked to Vaudeville theaters, often drawn by **23** there burlesque set **24** pieces, they featured scantily clad female performers. However, as theater promoters sought new opportunities, standard Vaudeville evolved into a more genteel version known as "Polite Vaudeville."

This new form of Vaudeville did not have any uniform structure, other than an eclectic set of acts mashed together under one playbill. Performances included musicians, singers, dancers, set-piece comedians, magicians, male and female impersonators, acrobats, jugglers, and occasionally one-act plays. Most of these forms **25** being interactive in nature, often provoking the audience to cheer or jeer at the performances and the performers. Importantly, Polite Vaudeville began to emphasize "family entertainment" as a marketing strategy. **26** The American family became important for Polite Vaudeville, and with that change, this form of theater also changed its focus.

23
A) NO CHANGE
B) its
C) it's
D) their

24
A) NO CHANGE
B) pieces, some of them featured
C) pieces, which featuring
D) pieces, which featured

25
A) NO CHANGE
B) are
C) were
D) were to be

26
The writer is considering deleting the underlined sentence. Should the writer do this?
A) Yes, because it merely reformulates the thought in the previous sentence.
B) Yes, because it directly contradicts the writer's point about Polite Vaudeville.
C) No, because it sets up the argument that will follow.
D) No, because it introduces an additional difference between older Vaudeville and Polite Vaudeville.

CONTINUE

[27] As the audience transitioned into this parents-with-children demographic, many performances took the lionization of the American Dream as their topic. Illustrating and celebrating the theme of upward mobility through individual hard work, [28] and defeating all odds, most set pieces for Polite Vaudeville had to be "peppy" with an often superficial struggle of a protagonist. [29] Then, the hero would rise to the occasion, overcome an arbitrary and trivial obstacle, and then go on to save his family, his farm, or some other cherished aspect of his life.

These performances were (and are) easy to criticize, since they promised victory and relief to Americans who faced harsh social and economic conditions on a daily basis. However, some rare Vaudeville performances were more political and took derisive jabs at the institutions that [30] emulated the American Dream. Irrespective of their specific content and its virtues, Polite Vaudeville performances all invited audiences to think, comment, and even participate.

27

Which choice most effectively transitions from the previous paragraph and introduces the information that follows?

A) NO CHANGE

B) As a result of the economic struggles most Americans faced,

C) Despite the shift in audience from adults to families,

D) Largely due to the influence of the government,

28

A) NO CHANGE

B) most set pieces for Polite Vaudeville had to be "peppy," featuring the often superficial struggle of a protagonist who defeats all odds.

C) a protagonist and a superficial struggle to defeat all odds often were featured in these "peppy" set pieces for Polite Vaudeville.

D) most set pieces for Polite Vaudeville, "peppy" and featuring an often superficial struggle of a protagonist defeating all odds.

29

A) NO CHANGE

B) Typically,

C) Consequently,

D) Nevertheless,

30

A) NO CHANGE

B) helped

C) achieved

D) perpetuated

But **31** all that would not last. Some *dramaturges* **32** suggest that, as cinema's popularity **33** promulgated, the interactive nature of performances like those of Polite Vaudeville declined. This theatrical ebb led to a disconnect between the audience and the performance, replacing what was once engaging theater with the spectacle of movie-goers passively staring at a celluloid screen.

31

The writer wants to more specifically identify what changed about entertainment in America. Which choice best accomplishes this goal?

A) that style of theater

B) the cynical and jaded attitude of the audience

C) the prevalence of audience involvement

D) disaffection with the American Dream

32

At this point, the writer is considering adding the following information.

—theater experts—

Should the writer make this addition here?

A) Yes, because it defines an obscure term in the sentence.

B) Yes, because it illustrates the reason for the change.

C) No, because it interrupts the flow of the sentence by supplying irrelevant information

D) No, because it weakens the focus of the passage by discussing a subject other than Polite Vaudeville.

33

A) NO CHANGE

B) grew

C) fostered

D) opened

CONTINUE

Questions 34-44 are based on the following passage.

A High-Tech Helping Hand

For a person who is missing a limb due to illness, accident, or a congenital condition, a prosthetic limb is a tool for independent living. Modern prosthetics can be highly specialized to fit the needs of specific wearers, and the expertise of biomedical engineers is fundamental to prosthetic limb design.

Conventional prosthetic limbs require careful measurements of an individual patient to ensure that the device fits the body as [34] closer than possible. Engineers have typically been concerned [35] for aspects of prosthetics such as the weight and function of artificial joints. Lightweight design is essential for prosthetic limbs because they contain no muscles of their own and require extra effort from remaining muscles to [36] move, such exertions can be tiring for the wearer. Some prosthetic limbs are controlled through [37] will power and frequent practice. For example, an artificial hand can grip an object through the manipulation of shoulder muscles. While these types of devices have their merits, they [38] clearly do not resemble true human parts.

Modern technological advancements are allowing engineers to experiment with more precise and sophisticated devices. Biomedical engineers who understand the neuromuscular structures of the body [39] has developed ways to link a device

34
A) NO CHANGE
B) closely for
C) close as
D) closely as

35
A) NO CHANGE
B) with
C) on
D) about

36
A) NO CHANGE
B) move, these
C) move; and such
D) move; such

37
Which choice provides the most relevant detail?
A) NO CHANGE
B) careful movement of distant muscle groups.
C) vigorous exercise of a single limb.
D) electromagnetic impulses from the brain.

38
Which choice best sets up the topic of the following paragraph?
A) NO CHANGE
B) have not been seriously considered by engineers.
C) can also be less precise than some users would like.
D) are also prone to malfunction and breakage.

39
A) NO CHANGE
B) had developed
C) have developed
D) developing

and  <u>its</u> wearer without relying on external motors or cables that respond to more distant muscles. Myoelectric prosthetic devices respond to the electrical impulses in the muscles of a truncated limb, which in some cases are still able to contract as though the limb were intact. Based on this electrical activity, the artificial limb can move naturally.

One challenge facing engineers in prosthetics research and development is how to provide nervous system feedback on a prosthetic limb's activity. 41 <u>Human limbs can quickly register information about temperature and texture, and this kind of sensory information is what allows a person to shake someone's hand without crushing it or to hold a cup without letting it fall.</u> In response to such considerations, biomedical engineers are conducting new research to test prosthetic limbs that, in addition to listening 42 <u>to the bodys'</u> electrical impulses to detect whether and how to move, can also give feedback to the body the way an organic limb does. 43 <u>It</u> would use electrical activity to tell the brain how much pressure an artificial limb is exerting on an object. A biomedical engineer 44 <u>that works</u> on such advanced prosthetic limbs is naturally required to work closely with users to identify needs and to test out possible solutions; only through subtlety and sensitivity will a new and improved generation of prosthetic devices be developed.

40
A) NO CHANGE
B) its'
C) it's
D) their

41
The writer is considering deleting the underlined sentence. Should the sentence be kept or deleted?
A) Kept, because it highlights the superiority of natural body systems.
B) Kept, because it details an ability that the engineers are attempting to recreate in prosthetic limbs.
C) Deleted, because it undermines the writer's notion that all capabilities can be recreated in prosthetic limbs.
D) Deleted, because it merely provides experimental details that are not relevant to this paragraph.

42
A) NO CHANGE
B) to the bodies
C) at the body's
D) to the body's

43
A) NO CHANGE
B) This technology
C) They
D) The scientists

44
A) NO CHANGE
B) works
C) working
D) will work

STOP

If you finish before time is called, you may check your work on this section only.
Do not turn to any other section.

No Test Material On This Page

Answer Key: TEST 4

Test 4

READING: SECTION 1

PASSAGE 1	**PASSAGE 2**	**PASSAGE 3**	**PASSAGE 4**	**PASSAGE 5**
Fiction	Social Science	Natural Science 1	Global Conversation	Natural Science 2
1. C	11. D	21. C	31. A	42. C
2. B	12. D	22. C	32. C	43. B
3. A	13. B	23. A	33. A	44. A
4. C	14. C	24. D	34. D	45. C
5. A	15. D	25. C	35. A	46. B
6. C	16. A	26. A	36. B	47. D
7. D	17. C	27. B	37. B	48. A
8. C	18. B	28. C	38. D	49. B
9. B	19. C	29. C	39. C	50. C
10. D	20. D	30. C	40. B	51. D
			41. C	52. C

GRAMMAR: SECTION 2

PASSAGE 1	**PASSAGE 2**	**PASSAGE 3**	**PASSAGE 4**
The Digital Generation	Cognitive Science Comes of Age	The Rise and Fall of Vaudeville	A High-Tech Helping Hand
1. B	12. C	23. D	34. D
2. D	13. A	24. D	35. B
3. C	14. B	25. C	36. D
4. D	15. C	26. A	37. B
5. A	16. D	27. A	38. C
6. A	17. A	28. B	39. C
7. B	18. C	29. B	40. A
8. C	19. C	30. D	41. B
9. D	20. A	31. C	42. D
10. C	21. B	32. A	43. B
11. B	22. B	33. B	44. C

Once you have determined how many questions
you answered correctly, consult the chart on Page 156
to determine **your scaled SAT Verbal score.**

Please visit **ies2400.com/ answers** for answer explanations.

Post-Test Analysis

This post-test analysis is essential if you want to see an improvement on your next test. Possible reasons for errors on the Reading and Grammar passages in this test are listed here. Place check marks next to the types of errors that pertain to you, or write your own types of errors in the blank spaces.

TIMING AND ACCURACY

◇ Spent too long reading individual passages
◇ Spent too long answering each question
◇ Spent too long on a few difficult questions
◇ Felt rushed and made silly mistakes or random errors
◇ Unable to work quickly using error types and POE
Other: _____

APPROACHING THE PASSAGES AND QUESTIONS

◇ Unable to effectively grasp a passage's tone or style
◇ Unable to effectively grasp a passage's topic or stance
◇ Did not understand the context of line references or underlined portions
◇ Did not eliminate false answers using strong evidence
◇ Answered questions using first impressions instead of POE
◇ Answered questions without checking or inserting final answer
◇ Eliminated correct answer during POE
Other: _____

> **Use this form** to better analyze your performance. If you don't understand why you made errors, there is no way that you can correct them!

READING TEST: # CORRECT_____   # WRONG _____   # OMITTED _____

◇ Interpreted passages rather than working with evidence
◇ Used outside knowledge rather than working with evidence
◇ Unable to effectively identify a passage's purpose or argument
◇ Unable to work effectively with word in context questions
◇ Unable to work effectively with questions about structure and writing technique
◇ Unable to work accurately or efficiently with Command of Evidence questions
◇ Unable to draw logical conclusions based on the content of the passages
◇ Difficulties understanding graphics and relating them to the passages
Other: _____

GRAMMAR TEST: # CORRECT_____   # WRONG _____   # OMITTED _____

◇ Did not identify proper verb number, form, or tense
◇ Did identify proper pronoun agreement or pronoun form (subject/object, who/which/where)
◇ Did not test for proper comparison phrasing (amount/number, between/among)
◇ Did not test phrase for correct adverb/adjective usage
◇ Did not see broader sentence structure (parallelism, misplaced modifier)
◇ Did not see flaws in punctuation (colon, semicolon, comma splice, misplaced commas)
◇ Did not see tricky possessives or contractions (its/it's, your/you're)
◇ Did not identify flaws in standard phrases (either . . . or, not only . . . but also, etc.)
◇ Did not use proper phrasing in sentences requiring the subjunctive
◇ Did not notice wordiness, redundancy, or faulty idioms
◇ Did not notice excessively informal expressions or flaws in essay style
◇ Created the wrong relationship between two sentences or two paragraphs
◇ Created the wrong placement for an out-of-order paragraph
◇ Did not properly read or analyze an insertion/deletion question
◇ Did not properly read or analyze the information in a graphic
◇ Understood a graphic, but could not identify the correct passage content
Other: _____

Test 5

Reading Test

65 MINUTES, 52 QUESTIONS

Turn to Section 1 of your answer sheet to answer the questions in this section.

DIRECTIONS

Each passage or pair of passages below is followed by a number of questions. After reading each passage or pair, choose the best answer to each question based on what is stated or implied in the passage or passages and in any accompanying graphics (such as a table or graph).

Questions 1-10 are based on the following passage.

This passage is adapted from a 2012 novella; the narrator is a teacher originally from the United Kingdom.

Twenty years ago, I was a teacher of English at Saint Andrew's School in Malawi, one of the smallest and poorest countries in Africa. The school occupied a large estate set
Line back from the road leading from the city of Blantyre to
5 Ndirande, a huddled township squeezed between the flanks of a mountain. The school buildings were solid and modern, the sports facilities were spacious and featured a large swimming pool. The students were the children of expatriates. Malawian children were educated, if at all, in villages, in the shade of
10 baobab trees.

I had been in the country just four weeks when I was invited on a trip to the very southernmost tip of the country, to Sucoma. There was a small private reserve there which, occasionally, hosted selected visitors. We met in the late
15 afternoon warmth: me, the headmaster and his wife, and the geography teacher and his wife, who was a native Malawian. Gripping her hand was a small girl gazing up in awe and silence at the white adults.

"This is Twambi, my niece," said the wife of the geography
20 teacher.

"Here with you on a visit?" asked the headmaster's wife.

"No. My sister's husband died and she has three other children. So Twambi is with us. She only speaks Chichewa."

"Oh. *Bwanji*[1], Twambi." The headmaster took off his hat
25 and bowed solemnly.

Twambi giggled and hid her face in her aunt's skirt. We piled into the jeep and set off on what turned out to be a three-hour, dusty, jolting drive along a deserted road which, more often than not, showed traces of tarmac. We arrived at the edge
30 of the reserve as dusk was falling. We were brought to the lodges where we would spend the night, given a simple meal, and then shown to bed, for we were to wake at half past four in the morning in order to reach the hide beside the water hole before daybreak.

35 In the morning, the company's truck dropped us about half a mile from our destination and we made our way through the surprisingly chilly darkness and silence until we arrived. The hide was built on stilts and an alarmingly rickety ladder allowed us access to it. We sat beneath the thatched roof on tall stools
40 and leaned forward to rest our elbows on the wooden shelf that ran the length of the structure. We peered through an opening, gazing at the clearing a few yards away. There lay the still water of the water hole. On the far edge of the pool was a sandy shore. Large trees framed the scene.

45 Stillness and silence. We held our breath intently. A rustle in the undergrowth and in procession small deer—nyala, perhaps—picked their way, delicately, to the water's edge and dipped their heads. Above them, an owl eased through the air and posed itself upon a heavy branch. The placid
50 bird hooted softly. A heron, white and stately, as if by magic (for we had not seen it enter the scene) stood as rigid as a sentinel, and a fish eagle floated through the lightening air. The nyala paused, raised their heads, then turned and moved away through the bushes. They were replaced by other deer.
55 A hammerkopf[2] called from the bushes, and this call seemed to be a cue, for a single line of warthogs, each with its tail pointing directly to the sky, trotted, almost comically, to the drinking place.

I do not remember all the animals we saw, although the
60 Malawian guide with us whispered the name of each animal or bird that took its turn at the water's edge. The light strengthened. It was as if a climactic moment were approaching. A group of female kudu came down to the pool and drank. Then, in unison,

CONTINUE ➡

they raised their heads and moved aside. At the top of the
65 slope, silhouetted against the dawn, stood an adult male kudu.
His head, raised proudly, showed off his towering, twisted,
powerful horns. He stared across the pool, directly at the hide.
Then, like royalty, he moved down to the pool, lowered his
head, and drank. He raised his eyes, stared across the pool at
70 us again, then turned and exited. The stage was bare. The sun
had risen.

1 "Bwanji" means "Hello" in Chichewa, the native language of Malawi

2 A medium-sized brown stork native to Africa

1

As used line 28, "jolting" most nearly means

A) surprising.
B) bumpy.
C) invigorating.
D) awakening.

2

According to the passage, the author was in Malawi to

A) teach native Malawian children.
B) work at a modern school.
C) experience Malawian culture.
D) observe local wildlife.

3

It can most reasonably be inferred from the passage that
the reserve in Sucoma

A) has multiple water holes.
B) welcomes international support.
C) is not open to the entire public.
D) belongs to Saint Andrew's School.

4

Which choice provides the best evidence for the answer
to the previous question?

A) Lines 1-3 ("Twenty . . . Africa")
B) Lines 13-14 ("There was . . . visitors")
C) Lines 42-43 ("There . . . hole")
D) Line 45 ("Stillness . . . intently")

5

The author uses the word "scene" in line 44 and the word
"stage" in line 70 in order to

A) imply that watching the animals at the water hole is like
watching a show.
B) suggest that a documentary could be made about the
water hole.
C) hint that a moment of high drama is about to occur.
D) emphasize the untouched wildness of the Sucoma
reserve.

6

According to the passage, the geography teacher's wife
has brought along a young girl who

A) has no living parent.
B) has suffered a loss.
C) is bilingual.
D) knows much about animals.

7

As used in line 70, "bare" most nearly means

A) devoid of activity.
B) inhospitable to life.
C) obvious.
D) unadorned.

8

It can be most reasonably inferred from the passage that a
"hide" is

A) a large plot of land with diverse wildlife.
B) a type of water hole frequented by birds and mammals.
C) a place specifically built for observation.
D) an emergency shelter made of wood.

CONTINUE ➤ 129

9

Which choice provides the best evidence for the answer to the previous question?

A) Lines 11-13 ("I had been . . . Sucoma")

B) Lines 30-34 ("We were . . . daybreak")

C) Lines 39-42 ("We sat . . . yards away")

D) Lines 50-52 ("A heron . . . air")

10

The purpose of the last paragraph is to

A) dramatize the entrance and exit of the male kudu.

B) illustrate that the male kudu is larger than average.

C) suggest that the male kudu maintains order at the water hole.

D) imply that the guide misunderstands the male kudu's behavior.

Questions 11-21 are based on the following passage and supplementary material.

This passage considers how cities, in particular the city of New York, are shaped by their approaches to new attractions and entertainment centers.

Staten Island: Tourist Destination. That, in a nutshell, is the rationale behind the most ambitious construction and engineering project to grace the least-visited of New York's
Line Five Boroughs. As I write, assembly is underway on the New
5 York Wheel, a 630 foot-tall Ferris wheel that could give Staten Island a new identity and its businesses a new stream of tourist-provided cash. That's if the plan works out, which for good reason it may not.

I hope, though, that the New York Wheel lives up to the
10 enormous expectations of the people who have conceived it, funded it, and believed in it. If successful, it will become a leisure destination like few others: visitors will ride the wheel in compartments large enough to house birthday parties and small corporate gatherings. There is some anticipation that in
15 the years to come more people will visit the Wheel than will visit the Statue of Liberty—which would mean that there will be at least 3.5 million new annual visitors to Staten Island. (Well, at least there's enough anticipation that Staten Island has built a new four-story parking garage.) Finally, something other
20 than the enjoyable but low-key Staten Island Ferry will define the Borough.

So why am I pessimistic? As an expert in urban studies (and a lifelong New Yorker), I have learned a thing or two about how the best-laid plans of the tourism and entertainment
25 industries can go awry. Where attractions are concerned, there is no such thing as "too big to fail." In fact, when you look at New York's recent history of entertainment and development, the real rule of thumb should be something like "small enough to succeed."
30 Let's return to Staten Island for a minute. Right now, the best reason to visit the Borough isn't an attraction or a historic site or an entertainment center, though I have always had a soft spot for the Staten Island Children's Museum. Instead, perhaps the best reason to stop off in Staten Island
35 is a bar and restaurant called the Phunky Elephant. Here you'll find a spacious dining room, live music, and a quirky, irresistible menu: I always get the charred corn salad and the house rigatoni with wild boar ragout. Few people know about the Phunky Elephant, but those who do feel uniquely and
40 justifiably privileged.

The problem with the New York Wheel is simply that: everybody is going to know about it, and nobody is going to feel privileged to know it. It is often said that we are living in a knowledge economy, where the aptness of one's connections
45 and the specialness of one's information are more important than the usual criteria of economic power—money and

CONTINUE

visibility. Something of the same sort has happened with urban planning in the past twenty years: the sites and spectacles that define the urban entertainment experience and draw some
50 of the most respectable profits are, in large part, insider's weapons. And everyone has a different one.

Today, if you go to the most dramatically reinvented of all New York's Boroughs—Brooklyn—you won't find particularly many postcard-ready sights. You will find small
55 boutiques, distinctive street fairs, idiosyncratic art galleries, and a restaurant scene of unparalleled vibrancy. Jersey City, Hoboken, and parts of Newark have revitalized themselves using similar fragment-and-conquer approaches. A Staten Island with a 630-foot wheel will give us something to stop and
60 photograph. Will it give us anything to discover, anything like the wonderfully localized and diversified paths to experience that are part of every successful 21st-century city?

Year	Projected New York Wheel Visitors (millions)	Projected Statue of Liberty Visitors (millions)
2016	2.00	3.00
2017	3.00	4.00
2018	4.00	5.00
2019	5.00	4.00
2020	5.00	4.00
2021	5.00	6.00

11

The main purpose of the passage is to

A) point out the drawbacks to an ambitious construction project.

B) develop a theory on how to revitalize blighted urban centers.

C) establish guidelines for creating future tourist attractions in Staten Island.

D) dispel myths regarding the role of urban planning in the infrastructure of New York's Five Boroughs.

12

The second paragraph functions to

A) subtly mock those who believe in the potential of current Staten Island attractions.

B) counter claims that the New York Wheel's construction will generate an insufficient return on its investment.

C) provide an outline of the hoped-for benefits of the Wheel's construction.

D) argue that the Wheel will attract crowds that Staten Island's infrastructure cannot presently accommodate.

13

The tone of the parenthetical observation in lines 18-19 is best characterized as

A) wry.

B) dismayed.

C) nostalgic.

D) upbeat.

14

The author mentions the Staten Island Children's Museum (line 33) in order to provide

A) an example of a widely-loved tourist attraction.

B) a best-case outcome for a large public works project.

C) an expression of a personal preference.

D) an instance of successful urban renewal.

15

As used in lines 40 and 43, "privileged" most nearly means

A) gifted.

B) wealthy.

C) exceptional.

D) confidential.

16

According to the passage, the New York Wheel could be unsuccessful because

A) nobody will want to take the Staten Island Ferry to ride it.

B) few people outside New York will know that it exists.

C) it will lack the allure of being a little-known attraction.

D) it will not feature the appealing hospitality of nearby destinations such as Jersey City and Hoboken.

17

Which choice provides the best evidence for the answer to the previous question?

A) Lines 11-14 ("If successful . . . gatherings")

B) Lines 25-26 ("Where attractions . . . to fail")

C) Lines 41-43 ("The problem . . . know it")

D) Lines 58-60 ("A Staten Island . . . photograph")

18

Which urban project would the author most strongly support as a means of attracting new tourists?

A) A monumental brass memorial in the style of the Statue of Liberty.

B) A strip of small but well-publicized restaurants specializing in eclectic dishes.

C) A giant outdoor art gallery meant to showcase paintings and handicrafts from all over the world.

D) A variety of small vendors, street performers, and cultural events.

19

Which choice provides the best evidence for the answer to the previous question?

A) Lines 14-17 ("There is . . . Staten Island")

B) Lines 30-33 ("Right now . . . Museum")

C) Lines 35-38 ("Here you'll . . . boar ragout")

D) Lines 54-56 ("You will . . . vibrancy")

20

According to the projected data in the table, which year confirms the claim that more people will visit the New York Wheel than will visit the Statue of Liberty?

A) 2016

B) 2017

C) 2019

D) 2021

21

Do the data in the table provide support for the "anticipation" (line 14) of annual visitors to Staten Island?

A) Yes, because the New York Wheel estimate would be proportional to estimates for other Staten Island attractions.

B) Yes, because the estimates of annual visitors to each location listed are inversely proportional.

C) No, because the data suggest that Staten Island will see more than 3.5 million new visitors to its major attractions in 2019 and subsequent years.

D) No, because the Statue of Liberty is expected to become more popular than the New York Wheel by 2021.

CONTINUE

Questions 22-32 are based on the following passage and supplementary material.

The author of this passage is an environmentalist and biologist who specializes in ocean and waterway ecosystems.

The threat of invasion has always loomed large in the human imagination. For hundreds of years, the possibility of invading armies attacking towns and cities was a real and ever-
Line present danger. In contemporary culture, the fear of invasion
5 has shifted towards the fantastical, with films, books, and television programs offering horrifying representations of a world overrun by zombies or aliens. By comparison, a species of freshwater fish hardly seems like a terrifying threat. Asian carp, however, pose a substantial risk to the ecological and
10 socio-economic wellbeing of the Great Lakes region.

"Asian carp" is a label applied to four distinct species: bighead, silver, grass, and black carp. All of these species originated in rivers in China and Russia. In the 1970s, Asian carp were transported to the southern United States and
15 introduced into ponds in hopes that they would help to control algae, plants, and snails. When flooding occurred, the fish were able to move from the ponds to small streams, and from those streams into the Mississippi River. The Mississippi was a carp paradise: it offered abundant food and no natural predators. As
20 a result, the population of Asian carp increased rapidly. The different species have been moving steadily northwards ever since.

So far, the influence that Asian carp have exerted on aquatic ecosystems reveals the threats these fish pose. Able
25 to eat up to 20% of their body weight per day, they consume huge masses of plankton and aquatic plants. One effect of this voracity is obvious: there is less food left for other aquatic species, and rapid population declines for other fish result. Other effects are more insidious: when the amount of aquatic
30 plant matter is depleted, other species can no longer rely on plants to offer concealment from predators, or to serve as safe nurseries for eggs and spawn. Asian carp, on the other hand,

tend to breed very successfully and can rapidly increase their numbers. They reduce biodiversity (in some areas, Asian carp
35 now comprise up to 80% of the total fish population) and can also introduce new diseases and parasites.

It is clear that Asian carp pose a significant threat to the wellbeing of aquatic ecosystems. What is less apparent, but equally important to consider, the potential impact on
40 human welfare. While Asian carp vary widely in size, some, especially the silver carp species, can grow to weigh up to 90 pounds. This species also displays a dangerous behavior when threatened: if startled, a silver carp will often leap into the air, sometimes attaining a height of close to 9 feet. If a fish of that
45 size were to strike a person, especially at high velocity, serious injuries would result. This kind of injury is less bloody and dramatic than the shark attacks that spring to mind when we think of dangerous fish, but the frequent use of the Great Lakes for recreation means that a significant Asian carp population
50 would create a high risk of injury. If recreational usage of the lakes for activities such as boating and water-skiing were to decrease as a result, a ripple effect would reach industries such as tourism and lead to declining employment.

Because of all these threats, a number of concerned
55 individuals are actively countering the spread of Asian carp into the Great Lakes ecosystem. There are two ways by which Asian carp could enter the Great Lakes: they could spread through waterways or be introduced by human activity. The former possibility is being combated through close monitoring
60 of areas with known Asian carp populations, especially during flooding, when it is easier for the fish to move into the streams and rivers that drain into the lakes. Risk reduction also hinges on eliminating the possibility that carp imported for food or as pets will be released into the wild. Legislation exists in the
65 Great Lakes region that prohibits the transportation, sale, or possession of live Asian carp. Anyone who finds an Asian carp is required to report the fish's presence. Just as posting a guard atop a castle can ensure that distant invaders are sighted, this strategy aims to ensure that any Asian carp presence is noticed
70 immediately—before a risk evolves.

Great Lakes Vacation Industry and Carp Population

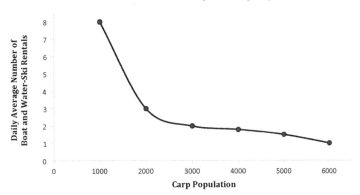

22

The first paragraph serves mainly to

A) summarize a problem and suggest a solution that will later be analyzed and encouraged.

B) provide an overview of the behavior of Asian carp in various environments.

C) inform the reader of the physical appearance and origins of Asian carp.

D) introduce an example of a concept that will be discussed in depth over the course of the passage.

23

According to the passage, Asian carp

A) were initially released into ponds as a solution to unwanted plant and animal growth.

B) were accidentally introduced into the Great Lakes area by means of trading boats from China.

C) were scarce in population in their native ecosystems but became ruthless predators in America.

D) were abundant yet benign in their native habitats, where they coexisted with many other species of fish.

24

Which choice provides the best evidence for the answer to the previous question?

A) Lines 1-4 ("The threat . . . danger")

B) Lines 13-16 ("In the 1970s . . . and snails")

C) Lines 23-26 ("So far . . . plants")

D) Lines 40-43 ("While Asian . . . threatened")

25

As used in line 37, "pose" most nearly means

A) cause.

B) present.

C) suggest.

D) arrange.

26

The author indicates that the growing population of Asian carp is harmful to native fish species because

A) the carp overcrowd ponds and lakes to the extent that some fish have stopped breeding as a result.

B) the carp are vicious carnivores that prey on small fish inhabiting the Great Lakes region.

C) the carp have discouraged environmental protection efforts in carp-dominated areas.

D) the carp deplete ecosystems of resources that other species use for food and protection.

27

Which choice provides the best evidence for the answer to the previous question?

A) Lines 4-8 ("In . . . threat")

B) Lines 18-22 ("The Mississippi . . . ever since")

C) Lines 27-31 ("there is . . . predators")

D) Lines 49-53 ("a significant . . . employment")

28

As used in line 62-63, "hinges on" most nearly means

A) is proved by.

B) is closely tied to.

C) takes into consideration that.

D) is defined by.

29

The author mentions "a guard atop a castle" (lines 67-68) primarily in order to

A) explain the defensive strategies adopted by the carp using an unexpected metaphor.

B) create a contrast between the carp and the individuals who are working to eliminate them.

C) illustrate the way in which some people plan to reduce the carp population by making a comparison.

D) emphasize the discretion and urgency of scientists working to remove carp from the Great Lakes.

CONTINUE

30

Which concept is supported by the passage and the information on the graph?

A) Asian carp are not only a threat to other animals in the Great Lakes region but also to the economic well-being of the area.

B) The growing population of Asian carp has come at the expense of plant and animal life in the Great Lakes.

C) Although scientists are aware of the threat Asian carp present to other fish, the danger that Asian carp present to humans has often been exaggerated.

D) While Asian carp can be detrimental to the safety of humans, they have nevertheless attracted new tourism to the Great Lakes.

31

How does the graph support the author's point that the carp population can also impact humans?

A) It demonstrates that the carp have become an unlikely but profitable tourist attraction.

B) It reveals that the number of humans attacked by carp is steadily increasing.

C) It shows that the growing number of carp has caused recreation activities in the Great Lakes to decline.

D) It illustrates that the increased population of carp has forced residents of the Great Lakes to migrate south.

32

Suppose the y-axis on the graph were to represent scuba gear rentals per day instead of boat and water ski rentals per day. Would this new graph support the author's claims?

A) Yes, because the author links growing carp populations to an overall decrease in water-based recreational activities.

B) Yes, because the author argues that water-based recreation can eventually adapt to larger carp populations.

C) No, because activities such as scuba diving would be more likely to disrupt Asian carp habitats.

D) No, because it is unclear to what extent the Great Lakes tourism industry profits from scuba gear rentals.

Questions 33-42 are based on the following passage.

The following passage is taken from *How the Other Half Lives* (1890), a book by social reformer Jacob Riis that describes the tenements of New York and their inhabitants.

Long ago it was said that "one half of the world does not know how the other half lives." That was true then. It did not know because it did not care. The half that was on top cared
Line little for the struggles, and less for the fate of those who were
5 underneath, so long as it was able to hold them there and keep its own seat. There came a time when the discomfort and crowding below were so great, and the consequent upheavals so violent, that it was no longer an easy thing to do, and then the upper half fell to inquiring what was the matter. Information on the subject
10 has been accumulating rapidly since, and the whole world has had its hands full answering for its old ignorance.

In New York, the youngest of the world's great cities, that time came later than elsewhere, because the crowding had not been so great. There were those who believed that it would never
15 come, but their hopes were vain. Greed and reckless selfishness wrought like results here as in the cities of older lands. "When the great riot occurred in 1863," so reads the testimony of the Secretary of the Prison Association of New York before a legislative committee appointed to investigate causes of the
20 increase of crime in the State twenty-five years ago, "every hiding-place and nursery of crime discovered itself by immediate and active participation in the operations of the mob. Those very places and domiciles, and all that are like them, are to-day nurseries of crime, and of the vices and disorderly courses which
25 lead to crime. By far the largest part—eighty per cent, at least— of crimes against property and against the person are perpetrated by individuals who have either lost connection with home life, or never had any, or whose homes had ceased to be sufficiently separate, decent, and desirable to afford what are regarded as
30 ordinary, wholesome influences of home and family. . . The younger criminals seem to come almost exclusively from the worst tenement house districts, that is, when traced back to the very places where they had their homes in the city here." Of one thing New York made sure at that early stage of the inquiry: the
35 boundary line of the Other Half lies through the tenements.

It is ten years and over, now, since that line divided New York's population evenly. Today three-fourths of its people live in the tenements, and the nineteenth century drift of the population to the cities is sending ever-increasing multitudes to
40 crowd them. The fifteen thousand tenant houses that were the despair of the sanitarian in the past generation have swelled into thirty-seven thousand, and more than twelve hundred thousand persons call them home. The one way out he saw—rapid transit to the suburbs—has brought no relief. We know now that there
45 is no way out; that the 'system' that was the evil offspring of public neglect and private greed has come to stay, a storm-center

forever of our civilization. Nothing is left but to make the best of a bad bargain.

50 What the tenements are and how they grow to what they are, we shall see hereafter. The story is dark enough, drawn from the plain public records, to send a chill to any heart. If it shall appear that the sufferings and the sins of the "other half," and the evil they breed, are but as a just punishment upon the community that gave it no other choice, it will be because that is the truth. The
55 boundary line lies there because, while the forces for good on one side vastly outweigh the bad—it were not well otherwise— in the tenements all the influences make for evil.

33

Riis describes the "half that was on top" (line 3) as interested in

A) maintaining its advantageous position.
B) alleviating the struggles of other people.
C) prolonging its ignorance of social issues.
D) provoking civil unrest in American cities.

34

As used in line 11, "old" most nearly means

A) experienced.
B) used.
C) former.
D) aged.

35

According to Riis, why did one half take interest in the lives of the other half?

A) Tenement residents began protesting inequality.
B) Sanitarians exposed the foul conditions in tenements.
C) Individuals in the city led humanitarian efforts.
D) Increasing violence and strife was difficult to ignore.

36

Which choice provides the best evidence for the answer to the previous question?

A) Lines 6-9 ("There came a time . . . the matter")
B) Lines 22-25 ("Those very . . . to crime")
C) Lines 40-43 ("The fifteen . . . them home")
D) Lines 54-57 ("The boundary . . . for evil")

37

Lines 25-33 ("By far . . . city here") suggest that crime is the product of an individual's

A) relationship with criminal relatives.
B) innate tendency to be violent.
C) jealousy of those who are more well-off.
D) upbringing in a deprived home.

38

Based on the passage, which choice best describes the "boundary line" (line 35)?

A) It is a police response to rampant crime in the city.
B) It marks the geographical center of the city.
C) It is the result of human selfishness and indifference.
D) It continues to evenly divide the city's population.

39

As used in line 38, "drift" most nearly means

A) bank.
B) migration.
C) implication.
D) tendency.

40

The passage indicates that concerned urban reformers had what hope?

A) Wealthy individuals would provide financial assistance to those living in tenements.
B) Expanding connections to areas outside city limits would alleviate overcrowding.
C) New York City would never become overcrowded.
D) Municipal laws would improve conditions in tenements.

CONTINUE

41

Which choice provides the best evidence for the answer to the previous question?

A) Lines 14-15 ("There were . . . vain")

B) Lines 30-33 ("The younger . . . city here")

C) Lines 43-44 ("The one . . . no relief")

D) Lines 47-48 ("Nothing is . . . bargain")

42

What main effect does the final paragraph have on the tone of the passage?

A) It creates a conversational tone, relating the struggle of tenement residents in everyday language.

B) It creates a somber tone, focusing on the bleak prospects of those who live in the tenements.

C) It creates an irrational tone, using language that describes housing as a form of evil.

D) It creates an ominous tone, relating the results of one sanitarian's research.

Questions 43-52 are based on the following passages.

In these readings, two authors consider recent developments in the study of speech and language skills.

Passage 1

The question of how our language shapes our thought processes has long puzzled scientists. Since the 1940s, various theories have been put forth in an attempt to show that those
Line who speak different languages quite literally see the world in
5 different ways. Yet no theorist has been able to definitively prove that it is language, rather than one's cultural background, that more directly impacts perception.

Psycholinguist Panos Athanasopoulos of Lancaster University hopes to settle the debate. In a cleverly designed
10 experiment, Athanasopoulos and his team worked with 15 participants. The first language of some participants is English; that of the rest is German. The choice of languages was intentional. English speakers tend to focus on what is happening in the present, rather than explicitly indicating
15 what has happened in the past, or what will happen in the future. For instance, it is not odd to say in English, "The woman is driving," but a German speaker would include more information: "The woman is driving to the store." As a result of these linguistic tendencies, Athanasopoulos predicted that
20 German speakers would be more "goal-oriented" in their thinking than English speakers.

To test his theory, Athanasopoulos had each of his participants view a video clip of someone walking, running, driving, or riding a bike. For each clip, the participants were
25 then asked to determine if a given scene with an ambiguous goal (for instance, a man walking towards a car that may or may not be his) was more similar to a scene with no clear goal (a man walking along a beach) or more similar to a scene with an obvious goal (a man walking into a post office).
30 Athanasopoulos found that English speakers only matched the ambiguous scenes with the goal-oriented scenes about 25% of the time, whereas the German speakers matched the ambiguous scenes with the goal-oriented scenes 40% of the time. The results are highly indicative that the native language of the
35 participants had a clear impact on the nature of the participants' perceptions.

Passage 2

According to John McWhorter, the idea that language influences cognition is nothing short of a "hoax." He has declared as much with the title of his most recent book, *The*
40 *Language Hoax: Why the World Looks the Same in Any Language* (2014), a quick read but a dense read, in certain respects. McWhorter, a scholar of linguistics at Columbia University, has declared that "Nothing has ever demonstrated that your language makes you process life in a different way. It

45 just doesn't work." *The Language Hoax* expands upon this idea example-by-example: for instance, "Japanese has a term that covers both green and blue. Russian has separate terms for dark and light blue. Does this mean that Russians perceive these colors differently from Japanese people?" For McWhorter, it
50 decidedly doesn't.

In certain respects, the idea that we all share the same language of cognition and observation is empowering. No human being on earth, under this theory, is shut off from a particular form of knowledge, expression, or emotion because
55 said human being happened to be born into the "wrong" language.

Yet McWhorter's ideas—and McWhorter himself seems to sense this—are not impervious to criticism. Consider the Russian language: unlike English, Russian does not contain
60 the articles "a" and "the"—a difference that is surely more consequential than a difference in shades of "blue." The most-studied divergences in language involve matters of structure rather than matters of naming: both a Russian and an American may see the same blue sky, but the habits of thought that each
65 uses to process and internalize this sight may be incompatible. It could be that language-based thought structures are simply too great to be overcome, not that they are relatively tiny factors, swamped by more universal habits of thought.

43

The primary role of the first paragraph of Passage 1 is to

A) cast doubt on a commonly held belief.

B) dispute a scientific principle.

C) redefine the parameters of a debate.

D) provide the theoretical context for an experiment.

44

As used in line 9, "settle" most nearly means

A) remedy.

B) rectify.

C) end.

D) suppress.

45

The description of Panos Athanasopoulos's experiment suggests that

A) culture has a strong effect on linguistic tendencies.

B) language influences how individuals assess specific situations.

C) country of birth is a strong indicator of an individual's willingness to make assumptions.

D) English and German have many similarities in terms of structure and vocabulary.

46

The author of Passage 2 would most likely respond to Panos Athanasopoulos's experiment with

A) disbelief, believing the methodology to be flawed.

B) skepticism, believing the link between lingual influences and behavior to be a fallacy.

C) support, believing language to be the most important determinant of an individual's behavior.

D) agreement, believing that differences in language structure may account for differences in thinking.

47

Which choice provides the best evidence for the answer to the previous question?

A) Lines 43-45 ("Nothing has . . . work")

B) Lines 46-50 ("for instance . . . doesn't")

C) Lines 57-58 ("Yet McWhorter's . . . criticism")

D) Lines 61-65 ("The most . . . incompatible")

48

The author of Passage 2 regards the prospect that language does not influence cognition as

A) depressing.

B) liberating.

C) unusual.

D) shocking.

CONTINUE

49

The example from *The Language Hoax* suggests that language does not influence cognition because

A) two languages can have the same word for one color but very different conceptions of that color.

B) two languages can have different words for different colors but the same opinion of those colors.

C) one language can be radically different from others, yet its speakers retain the ability to express their perceptions using other languages if they become fluent.

D) two languages can have different concepts of where one characteristic ends and another begins, yet speakers of both languages will perceive reality in the same way.

50

Which choice provides the best evidence for the answer to the previous question?

A) Lines 37-38 ("According to . . . hoax")

B) Lines 52-56 ("No human . . . language")

C) Lines 58-61 ("Consider the . . . blue")

D) Lines 66-68 ("It could . . . thought")

51

As used in line 68, "swamped" most nearly means

A) inundated.

B) overpowered.

C) beset.

D) saturated.

52

The last sentence of Passage 2 indicates that the author questions whether

A) all languages provide equally useful tools for critical thinking.

B) the debate between those who see language's influence on cognition as negligible and those who see it as critical will ever be resolved.

C) language is genuinely insignificant in the study of perception and cognition.

D) a comprehensive theory of human thought might be more important than theories that articulate the differences between individual languages.

STOP

If you finish before time is called, you may check your work on this section only.
Do not turn to any other section.

Writing Test
35 MINUTES, 44 QUESTIONS

Turn to Section 2 of your answer sheet to answer the questions in this section.

DIRECTIONS

Each passage below is accompanied by a number of questions. For some questions, you will consider how the passage might be revised to improve the expression of ideas. For other questions, you will consider how the passage might be edited to correct errors in sentence structure, usage, or punctuation. A passage or a question may be accompanied by one or more graphics (such as a table or graph) that you will consider as you make revising and editing decisions.

Some questions will direct you to an underlined portion of a passage. Other questions will direct you to a location in a passage or ask you to think about the passage as a whole.

After reading each passage, choose the answer to each question that most effectively improves the quality of writing in the passage or that makes the passage conform to the conventions of standard written English. Many questions include a "NO CHANGE" option. Choose that option if you think the best choice is to leave the relevant portion of the passage as it is.

Questions 1-11 are based on the following passage.

Low Visibility, High Wages

For many people, the words "high-salary job" bring to mind the **1** figure of doctors, lawyers, business executives, and international celebrities. **2** Far less people, upon hearing these same words, would think of air traffic controllers. However, in 2015, the average air traffic controller earned a salary of roughly $126,000, according to the jobs and employment statistics site Glassdoor.com. This number is comparable to the average salary for lawyers, **3** which was estimated at $131,000 in 2013.

1
A) NO CHANGE
B) figures of
C) figure with
D) figures with

2
A) NO CHANGE
B) Far lesser
C) Far fewer
D) Fewer by far

3
A) NO CHANGE
B) which they estimated
C) which being estimated
D) having estimated it

CONTINUE

Air traffic controllers are not the only professionals who earn considerable salaries while working more or less out of sight. (After all, when was the last time you saw a television drama about air traffic controllers?) In its current rankings of the "Best Paying Jobs," U.S. News and World Report lists both a fair number of expected careers (doctors, lawyers, software specialists) **4** despite a fair number of unexpected choices. Pharmacists, nurses, construction managers, and physical therapists are among the professionals who earn relatively high salaries **5** by expecting to see their chosen industries grow increasingly important in the years ahead. **6** Some of these industries also experienced remarkable, though short-lived, expansion during the 1990s.

Why exactly do individuals in these careers command such high wages? In many cases, employers are paying for valuable specialized knowledge and training and are selecting from an already small pool of talent. Air traffic controllers, for instance, must complete courses at the Federal Aviation Academy in order to begin work. **7** Surprisingly, without the expertise provided by air traffic controllers— **8** who will actually spend less time on their formal studies than some software engineers will—the day-to-day workings of major airlines would be imperiled.

4
A) NO CHANGE
B) including
C) beyond
D) and

5
A) NO CHANGE
B) which makes them expect
C) so that you expect
D) and who can expect

6
The writer is considering deleting the underlined sentence. Should the writer do this?
A) Yes, because it is not clear exactly what industries the writer could be referring to.
B) Yes, because the sentence detracts from the passage's emphasis on the job market during the past few years.
C) No, because the sentence offers an important exception to the writer's overall thesis.
D) No, because the sentence provides historical and economic context that is referenced in subsequent paragraphs.

7
A) NO CHANGE
B) In contrast,
C) Similarly,
D) Furthermore,

8
The writer wants to add detail that explains the practical duties of air traffic controllers. Which choice best accomplishes this goal?
A) NO CHANGE
B) who coordinate flights so that runway space is used efficiently and collisions do not occur
C) who hold themselves to the highest standards of attention to detail
D) who are respected by other air transit professionals, including airline pilots

[1] Granted, those who seek fame would probably not find work in air traffic control especially fulfilling: the workstations of many air traffic controllers are located in tall cement towers near airport runways, well removed from the public eye. [2] The same is true of many high-paying healthcare roles, since nurses, pharmacists, and physical therapists all **9** focus primarily on customers and patients, not on public relations or hot-button causes. [3] In today's economy, very few aspiring entertainers will attain the multimillion-dollar salaries of the Hollywood **10** elite, because few aspiring businessmen will achieve the multibillion-dollar net worth of magnates such as Bill Gates and Michael Bloomberg. [4] However, sometimes sacrificing opportunities for fame to opportunities for security is an excellent choice. [5] People who harbor such visions of fame and power still need to provide for themselves and their families on a day-to-day basis. [6] For these individuals, the best course in life may be to find a high-paying job that is rather predictable and out-of-the-way, but could impart the life skills and the sense of responsibility needed to reach for something bigger. **11**

9
A) NO CHANGE
B) apportion energy to
C) devote themselves to
D) are mostly about

10
A) NO CHANGE
B) elite, although few
C) elite; few
D) elite, few

11
To make this paragraph most logical, sentence 4 should be placed
A) where it is now.
B) before sentence 1.
C) before sentence 3.
D) before sentence 6.

CONTINUE

Questions 12-22 are based on the following passage.

Art in the Great Outdoors

Because I have always enjoyed the world of nature, I have often found museums to be cold and constricting. Growing up, I viewed class trips to museums as unpleasant ordeals: I [12] remember distinct one visit to the Museum of Modern Art in New York, when I refused to explore any of the indoor exhibitions and [13] planted myself on a bench in the sculpture garden until it was time to leave. [14] No matter how pristine, no matter how beautiful, museums induce a claustrophobia. I cannot overcome it, not even now that I have graduated from college.

[12]

A) NO CHANGE
B) remember direct
C) distinctly remember
D) remember directing

[13]

A) NO CHANGE
B) had planted
C) have planted
D) was planting

[14]

In context, which choice best combines the underlined sentences?

A) I cannot overcome it, even now that I have graduated from college, no matter how pristine, no matter how beautiful, museums induce a claustrophobia.

B) No matter how pristine, no matter how beautiful, museums induce a claustrophobia that I cannot overcome, not even now that I have graduated from college.

C) No matter how pristine, no matter how beautiful, museums induce a claustrophobia without overcoming it, not even now that I have graduated from college.

D) Museums induce a claustrophobia yet I cannot overcome it, not even now that I have graduated from college, no matter how pristine, no matter how beautiful.

[15] Until then, I discovered a few years ago that closed-in museums are not the only places where great art can be experienced. I was searching the Internet to plan a weekend trip [16] when I came across an advertisement for Grounds for Sculpture, which describes itself as "a 42-acre sculpture park and museum located in Hamilton Township, New Jersey." There are indoor exhibitions, [17] but, as I soon discovered these, are designed mostly to [18] compliment the major offerings in outdoor art, which grow "by approximately fifteen sculptures annually." My eventual visit did not disappoint: hills, trees, and flowers work in tandem with sculptures by both figurative and abstract artists to create a landscape of stirring beauty.

Grounds for Sculpture is not the only outdoor sculpture park in America. It did not take me long to discover another, similar attraction in my area of the country, the Storm King Art Center, which is located in New York State's Hudson Valley. This second "outdoor museum" is sprawling, almost sublime. Visit during the fall, and [19] visitors will find massive abstract sculptures [20] by Barnett Newman and David Smith in settings of rousing natural beauty; the fiery colors of autumn foliage accentuate the stark and powerful shapes of the artworks that populate Storm King.

15
A) NO CHANGE
B) In the past,
C) Fortunately,
D) Certainly,

16
A) NO CHANGE
B) where
C) in which
D) by which

17
A) NO CHANGE
B) but as I soon discovered these,
C) but as, I soon discovered, these
D) but, as I soon discovered, these

18
A) NO CHANGE
B) complement
C) complete
D) corroborate

19
A) NO CHANGE
B) you
C) one
D) the public

20
The writer is considering deleting the underlined phrase. Should the writer make this deletion?

A) Yes, because Barnett Newman and David Smith are not the only important artists featured at the Storm King Art Center.
B) Yes, because the artwork of Barnett Newman is not analyzed elsewhere in the passage.
C) No, because the reference to David Smith sets up the author's later discussion.
D) No, because the author expresses a preference for these artists earlier in the passage.

CONTINUE

I realize that some people may write off destinations such as Grounds for Sculpture and Storm King Art Center as gimmicky tourist attractions, places somehow "inferior" to more traditional museums. But those people couldn't be more wrong. After all, David Smith designed many of his metalwork sculptures specifically for outdoor display; **21** he even set up several of his creations in a field on his own property, in arrangements that recall the installations at Storm King. As I see it, sculpture parks such as the ones I admire serve valuable purposes. These attractions **22** agitate a new audience for art, winning over reluctant museum-goers such as myself. Just as importantly, these attractions help us to understand dimensions of great art that traditional museums may not be equipped to address. David Smith's sculptures should be surrounded by nature; let's visit them in their proper habitat.

21

Which choice provides information that best supports the claim made earlier in the sentence?

A) NO CHANGE
B) the curators at Storm King have had considerable success finding aesthetically pleasing arrangements for even his largest works.
C) among his favorite motifs are shapes that recall leaves and ferns, but that were crafted using stainless steel.
D) there is no logical reason why placing Smith's sculptures outdoors should compromise their status as celebrated works of art.

22

A) NO CHANGE
B) institute
C) constitute
D) create

Questions 23-33 are based on the following passage and supplementary material.

Going Crazy with MSG

Monosodium Glutamate (MSG) is an additive used to enhance the flavor of food. It has a reputation for being used most commonly in Chinese restaurant cuisine, and even spawned the idea of "Chinese Restaurant Syndrome," **23** it is a reaction to consumption of the ingredient. But many do not realize that MSG is also present in thousands of commonly packaged pantry items such as canned soups, flavored potato chips, and salad dressings. After World War II, this substance rose in popularity in the American market and developed a reputation for being detrimental to one's health. Some experts claim that daily ingestion of MSG can initiate headaches, depression, and fatigue—among other concerning effects. **24** To disassociate their dining experience from the MSG craze, both domestic and international restaurants have posted "No MSG" notices. These appear in their windows and even on their menus.

In an effort to combat this negative media attention, many scientists, aided by the Food and Drug Administration (FDA), **25** had worked to **26** dull the unsavory reputation of MSG. Functionally, MSG is the salt component of an amino acid called Glutamic Acid. Amino acids form proteins, and thus can be found naturally in foods containing protein. **27** Specifically, high levels of the amino acid Glutamate occur biologically in tomatoes, mushrooms, and Parmesan cheese.

23

A) NO CHANGE
B) being
C) that is
D) DELETE the underlined portion.

24

Which choice most effectively combines the underlined sentences?

A) Both domestic and international restaurants have posted "No MSG" notices in their windows and even on their menus, this strategy is employed to disassociate their dining experience from the MSG craze.
B) To disassociate their dining experience from the MSG craze, "No MSG" notices have been posted by both domestic and international restaurants in their windows and even on their menus.
C) To disassociate their dining experience from the MSG craze, both domestic and international restaurants have posted "No MSG" notices in their windows and even on their menus.
D) "No MSG" notices have been posted in the windows and even on the menus of both domestic and international restaurants to disassociate their dining experience from the MSG craze.

25

A) NO CHANGE
B) have worked
C) working
D) are going to be working

26

A) NO CHANGE
B) get done with
C) disqualify
D) dispel

27

A) NO CHANGE
B) However
C) Fortunately
D) Broadly speaking

CONTINUE

[1] So how did the regular use of MSG begin? [2] Japanese scientist Kikunae Ikeda first recognized MSG as a flavor enhancer in 1908 while creating soup stock out of seaweed that contained high MSG concentrations. [3] The substance now bought by companies and kitchens all across the United States is a clear crystal—like salt or sugar. [4] In some cases, misuse of the product may be to blame for adverse reactions. [5] If a restaurant [28] had sprinkled MSG on top of a dish, as opposed to mixing it in during cooking, a customer would ingest a whole serving in one bite. [6] He subsequently found a method of isolating the ingredient through bacterial fermentation, [29] patents the process, and begins producing MSG commercially. [7] This overexposure will tax the body and induce an adverse reaction, comparable to the reaction to consuming a high concentration of salt or sugar. [30]

28
A) NO CHANGE
B) were to sprinkle
C) will sprinkle
D) sprinkle

29
A) NO CHANGE
B) patenting the process, and began to produce
C) patented the process, and began producing
D) patented the process, and beginning produced

30
To make this paragraph most logical, sentence 6 should be placed
A) where it is now.
B) after sentence 1.
C) after sentence 2.
D) after sentence 3.

Unfortunately, scientists have stood in the way of an honest assessment of MSG. Neuroscientist John Olney's recent study, which involved injecting laboratory mice directly with MSG, only perpetuated MSG misconceptions. Proportionally, the quantities given to the mice would be fit for a horse rather than a human. Additionally, the substance was released under the skin while humans only introduce MSG to **31** its bodies via the digestive system. This "meticulous, double blind study" was conducted by scientists from reputable institutions around the world but only addressed the worst-case misuse of MSG that occurs in some restaurants. Furthermore, those who consumed the placebos in this study **32** reported symptoms as inconsistently as those ingesting the MSG—largely disproving any clear scientific basis for the MSG outcry. Olney's study does not legitimately prove that MSG is harmful, **33** yet the public continues to believe that MSG, rather than overeating, is responsible for mass discomfort.

31
A) NO CHANGE
B) it's
C) there
D) their

32
Which choice offers an accurate interpretation of the data in the graph?
A) NO CHANGE
B) were significantly less likely to experience symptoms than
C) experienced even higher rates of depression than
D) were marginally less susceptible to an increase in headaches than

33
The writer wants a conclusion that conveys how the flaws in John Olney's study have been overlooked by those in the restaurant industry. Which choice best accomplishes this goal?
A) NO CHANGE
B) and the FDA is currently working with restaurants to inform the public about MSG's harmful effects.
C) but those in the restaurant industry continue to liberally use MSG in their dishes.
D) and still, restaurateurs strive to distance themselves from the stigma of MSG.

Treatment Results of Individuals with MSG

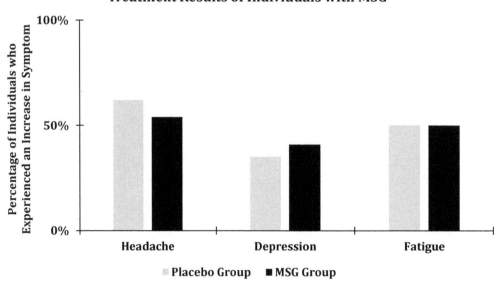

■ Placebo Group   ■ MSG Group

CONTINUE

Questions 34-44 are based on the following passage.

Save the Bananas!

— 1 —

Bananas are one of the world's largest fruit crops and are consumed in great volume in the United States. Of the many species that can be found in the wild, Cavendish bananas are most commonly cultivated and sold for human consumption. **34** These are the seedless, perfectly yellow variety that American shoppers have come to recognize on supermarket **35** shelves, they currently represent about forty-five percent of global banana production. All Cavendish bananas are in fact clones of one another. One side effect of this cloning is that Cavendish bananas do not have sufficient genetic variation to subsist in the face of major fungal or bacterial diseases.

34
A) NO CHANGE
B) This is
C) That is
D) That were

35
A) NO CHANGE
B) shelves they
C) shelves; they
D) shelves; it

— 2 —

However, this favorable resistance would only last until an old foe of the Cavendish took a new form. Tropical Race 4, an evolved strain of a disease that heavily affects the [36] Cavendish— surfaced in Asia in 1992. The fungus has slowly spread to the Philippines, Australia, and most recently Africa. [37] Nevertheless, Tropical Race 4 can live in the soil for decades and [38] will contaminate bananas as soon as they are re-introduced. Some prominent agricultural companies have implemented crop rotation as one method of managing the diseased soil. Growers who use this method will often plant a distinct crop with anti-fungal capabilities. Farmers in China have demonstrated the efficiency of this practice by alternately planting bananas and Chinese leeks on the same land.

[36]

A) NO CHANGE
B) Cavendish,
C) Cavendish;
D) Cavendish:

[37]

A) NO CHANGE
B) Consequently,
C) Moreover,
D) Regardless,

[38]

A) NO CHANGE
B) can contaminate
C) may contaminate
D) contaminating

CONTINUE

— 3 —

The Cavendish was cultivated as [39] a replacement for the previously popular banana species, the Gros Michel, which reigned supreme within American and European agricultural markets through the late 1950's. However, Panama Disease began spreading through Gros Michel crops in South America and the Caribbean [40] —creating a banana plague that almost bankrupted major importers of the crop. On account of its resistance to the incurable Panama disease, [41] growers resolved to adopt the Cavendish as the most comparable substitute in taste and appearance.

— 4 —

Still, developing strains of bananas that will be resistant to Tropical Race 4 is a more viable, collective solution. The Taiwan Banana Research Institute, for instance, cultivates tissue-culture plants and deposits them in soil thoroughly polluted with Tropical Race 4. Scientists form these engineered plant specimens by harvesting and cleaning healthy suckers [42] from existing banana plants. Disinfected pieces of the suckers are planted on a laboratory medium and made to grow several shoots. After assessing the shoots for known diseases and viruses, technicians discard those that test positive and prepare the problem-free specimens for planting.

39

A) NO CHANGE
B) replacements
C) replacing
D) having replaced

40

The writer is considering deleting the underlined portion (ending the sentence with a period). Should the writer make this deletion?

A) Yes, because it digresses from the main point of the paragraph.
B) Yes, because the information discussed is irrelevant to the passage as a whole.
C) No, because the underlined portion offers new insight into the causes of Panama Disease.
D) No, because the underlined portion provides information necessary to the paragraph's main idea.

41

A) NO CHANGE
B) the Cavendish was adopted by growers as
C) growers determined that the Cavendish was
D) Cavendish bananas are

42

At this point, the writer is considering adding the following parenthetical statement.

(lateral shoots of the underground stem)

Should the writer make this addition here?

A) Yes, because it demonstrates the writer's extensive knowledge of botany.
B) Yes, because it defines a term that is introduced in the paragraph.
C) No, because it is not necessary to the main point of the paragraph.
D) No, because it conflicts with points made elsewhere in the writer's discussion of cultivating banana tissue.

CONTINUE ➡　151

— 5 —

This meticulous selection and growth procedure **43** assures that the banana plants are free of harmful fungi and bacteria, which are harder to combat through crop rotation. It can also produce plants that exhibit slight variations from their mother plant, mutants like the Giant Cavendish banana. Generated by the Taiwan Banana Research Institute, the Giant Cavendish is much more resistant to Tropical Race 4 and may serve as a viable substitute for the common Cavendish banana.

Question 44 asks about the previous passage as a whole.

43

A) NO CHANGE
B) insures
C) ensures
D) reassures

Think about the previous passage as a whole as you answer question 44.

44

To make the passage most logical, paragraph 2 should be placed

A) where it is now.
B) before paragraph 1.
C) before paragraph 4.
D) before paragraph 5.

STOP

If you finish before time is called, you may check your work on this section only.
Do not turn to any other section.

No Test Material On This Page

Answer Key: TEST 5

Test 5

READING: SECTION 1

PASSAGE 1	PASSAGE 2	PASSAGE 3	PASSAGE 4	PASSAGE 5
Fiction	**Social Science**	**Natural Science 1**	**Global Conversation**	**Natural Science 2**
1. B	11. A	22. D	33. A	43. D
2. B	12. C	23. A	34. C	44. C
3. C	13. A	24. B	35. D	45. B
4. B	14. C	25. B	36. A	46. D
5. A	15. C	26. D	37. D	47. D
6. B	16. C	27. C	38. C	48. B
7. A	17. C	28. B	39. B	49. D
8. C	18. D	29. C	40. B	50. B
9. C	19. D	30. A	41. C	51. B
10. A	20. C	31. C	42. B	52. C
	21. D	32. A		

GRAMMAR: SECTION 2

PASSAGE 1	PASSAGE 2	PASSAGE 3	PASSAGE 4
Low Visibility, High Wages	**Art in the Great Outdoors**	**Going Crazy with MSG**	**Save the Bananas!**
1. B	12. C	23. D	34. A
2. C	13. A	24. C	35. C
3. A	14. B	25. B	36. B
4. D	15. C	26. D	37. C
5. D	16. A	27. A	38. B
6. B	17. D	28. B	39. A
7. D	18. B	29. C	40. D
8. B	19. B	30. C	41. B
9. A	20. C	31. D	42. B
10. C	21. A	32. A	43. C
11. C	22. D	33. D	44. C

Once you have determined how many questions
you answered correctly, consult the chart on Page 156
to determine **your scaled SAT Verbal score.**

Please visit ies2400.com/answers for answer explanations.

Post-Test Analysis

This post-test analysis is essential if you want to see an improvement on your next test. Possible reasons for errors on the Reading and Grammar passages in this test are listed here. Place check marks next to the types of errors that pertain to you, or write your own types of errors in the blank spaces.

TIMING AND ACCURACY

◇ Spent too long reading individual passages
◇ Spent too long answering each question
◇ Spent too long on a few difficult questions
◇ Felt rushed and made silly mistakes or random errors
◇ Unable to work quickly using error types and POE

Other: _____

APPROACHING THE PASSAGES AND QUESTIONS

◇ Unable to effectively grasp a passage's tone or style
◇ Unable to effectively grasp a passage's topic or stance
◇ Did not understand the context of line references or underlined portions
◇ Did not eliminate false answers using strong evidence
◇ Answered questions using first impressions instead of POE
◇ Answered questions without checking or inserting final answer
◇ Eliminated correct answer during POE

Other: _____

> **Use this form** to better analyze your performance. If you don't understand why you made errors, there is no way that you can correct them!

READING TEST: # CORRECT_____ # WRONG _____ # OMITTED _____

◇ Interpreted passages rather than working with evidence
◇ Used outside knowledge rather than working with evidence
◇ Unable to effectively identify a passage's purpose or argument
◇ Unable to work effectively with word in context questions
◇ Unable to work effectively with questions about structure and writing technique
◇ Unable to work accurately or efficiently with Command of Evidence questions
◇ Unable to draw logical conclusions based on the content of the passages
◇ Difficulties understanding graphics and relating them to the passages

Other: _____

GRAMMAR TEST: # CORRECT_____ # WRONG _____ # OMITTED _____

◇ Did not identify proper verb number, form, or tense
◇ Did identify proper pronoun agreement or pronoun form (subject/object, who/which/where)
◇ Did not test for proper comparison phrasing (amount/number, between/among)
◇ Did not test phrase for correct adverb/adjective usage
◇ Did not see broader sentence structure (parallelism, misplaced modifier)
◇ Did not see flaws in punctuation (colon, semicolon, comma splice, misplaced commas)
◇ Did not see tricky possessives or contractions (its/it's, your/you're)
◇ Did not identify flaws in standard phrases (either . . . or, not only . . . but also, etc.)
◇ Did not use proper phrasing in sentences requiring the subjunctive
◇ Did not notice wordiness, redundancy, or faulty idioms
◇ Did not notice excessively informal expressions or flaws in essay style
◇ Created the wrong relationship between two sentences or two paragraphs
◇ Created the wrong placement for an out-of-order paragraph
◇ Did not properly read or analyze an insertion/deletion question
◇ Did not properly read or analyze the information in a graphic
◇ Understood a graphic, but could not identify the correct passage content

Other: _____

New SAT Verbal: Scaled Scores

To obtain your scaled New SAT Verbal score, calculate the number of questions you answered correctly in Reading (Section 1) and Grammar (Section 2). Then, use the chart below to determine your scoring range.

Questions Correct	Scaled Score Range	Questions Correct	Scaled Score Range	Questions Correct	Scaled Score Range
96	800	64	570-550	32	400-380
95	800-780	63	560-550	31	390-380
94	780-770	62	560-540	30	390-370
93	760-750	61	550-540	29	380-370
92	750-740	60	550-530	28	380-370
91	740-730	59	540-530	27	380-360
90	730-710	58	540-520	26	380-360
89	710-700	57	530-520	25	370-360
88	710-700	56	530-510	24	370-350
87	700-690	55	520-510	23	370-350
86	700-690	54	520-500	22	360-350
85	690-680	53	510-500	21	360-340
84	680-670	52	510-490	20	350-340
83	670-660	51	500-490	19	350-330
82	660-650	50	500-490	18	340-330
81	660-640	49	490-480	17	340-320
80	640-630	48	490-470	16	330-310
79	640-630	47	480-470	15	330-310
78	630-620	46	480-460	14	320-300
77	630-630	45	470-460	13	320-290
76	620-610	44	460-450	12	310-290
75	620-610	43	460-440	11	300-280
74	610-600	42	450-440	10	300-280
73	610-600	41	450-440	9	290-270
72	610-600	40	440-430	8	290-260
71	600-590	39	440-420	7	270-260
70	600-580	38	430-420	6	270-250
69	590-580	37	430-410	5	260-230
68	590-570	36	420-410	4	240-210
67	580-570	35	410-400	3	220-200
66	580-560	34	410-390	2	210-200
65	570-560	33	400-390	1	200

Made in the USA
Las Vegas, NV
27 July 2021